Primordial Psyche:
A Reliving of the
Soul of Ancestors

A Jungian and
Transpersonal Worldview

Diego Pignatelli Spinazzola

iUniverse, Inc.
Bloomington

Primordial Psyche: A Reliving of the Soul of Ancestors
A Jungian and Transpersonal Worldview

iUniverse books may be ordered through booksellers or by contacting:

iUniverse
1663 Liberty Drive
Bloomington, IN 47403
www.iuniverse.com
1-800-Authors (1-800-288-4677)

ISBN: 978-1-4502-8456-1 (sc)
ISBN: 978-1-4502-8457-8 (ebk)

Printed in the United States of America

iUniverse rev. date: 3/16/2011

CONTENTS

AUTHOR'S PREFACE

This is a collection of articles and brief thoughts orientated towards Jungian and transpersonal analysis. I will examine the collection thematically and ask some fundamental philosophical questions relating to our age of crisis and transition.

This book is a summary of modern themes which aims to reflect Jungian and transpersonal thought re-interpreted through my personal key readings. These range from primitive psychologies and their relationship with *tremendum*, magic, magical and archaic thought currently re-evoked in psychosis, obsessive-compulsive rituals and personality disorders, prophetic and mystical visions, the meaning and re-evaluation of analytical psychology and its fascinating theories on archetypes of the collective unconscious, to the ancient Hindu Tantra and avatars: the disciples of the invisible who reflect the heroic destiny of "mythical saviours" and humanity's helpers.

Primordial psyche narrates the history of humanity and destiny with which have always clashed. Demons, exorcisms and occult fears which rage like ghosts in the psyche of modern man.

Primordial Psyche is also the story of how man has temporarily desacralized the nature of spiritual and mystic phenomena which are returning in another guise like unconscious, autonomous complexes (or so-called *daimons*) to persecute humanity and worm their way into ordinary madness and collective psychoses in an era of fragmentation and psychic poverty. We have something to learn from this psychic dissociation: if only an individual would bravely choose the heroic path of return to what is Ancient then he would be the creative bearer of a new civilization. By re-conquering his own Soul he will be reconnected to the *anima mundi* of ancient peoples.

The articles which follow are a creative attempt at a non-chronological, narrative summary of the mythologems (or leitmotifs or mythical themes) which humanity has passed through in the history of its archetypal phases. These are linked back to the collective unconscious; the phylogenetic deposit of a super-personal nature whose matrix goes back to myths and various primordial representations — the universal heritage of man's psychic history. We have gone beyond meta-narration. We find ourselves with a real possibility for man to redress the entire history of humanity in its mythical significance and to cure himself from his illegitimate, alienating and selfish conditions of a personalized escape from what is sacred. The hero journey which belongs to the creative individual who has the gift of an individual soul is not incompatible with the drive and the desire to transcend the whole of humanity.

The mythical origin amplifies this desire to transcend and extends it beyond the limits of the psyche and the universe. Primitive civilizations had subtle and elaborate means of connecting with the sacred. Even the Tantra are an exegetic system for accessing spiritual and mystical phenomena using elaborate procedures as will be seen in my observations on Indian philosophy and symbolism.

Spiritual techniques are dynamics for accessing the god inside each man. The mystic glimpsed the divine image in himself and in his body-mind. While conventional religions and sciences do all they can to extinguish an individual's *entheos* (literally: the god within) and its cosmic, super-individual status, modern psycho-dynamic and integrative, holistic therapies with the help of meditative techniques serve as amplifiers of the psyche and manage to rediscover and integrate this apparently lost identity.

But for conventional Christianity the remains of the divine in man are only the *imago dei*: a small glimmer or a fragment of the image of god. At this point I refer to two articles *Theory of Christian faith and a mystic's prophetic soul* and *the individual soul and humanity's destiny*. These articles refer back to the Jung's (1960) interpretation of experience and the religious function of the soul ("*anima naturaliter religiosa*".

I then return to the myth which shows the primordial beginnings of man, before autonomous and differentiated consciousness was born and standardized as in today's culture. I invite the reader to understand a message which in combination with the Jungian vision could augur a new dialectic synthesis of a reciprocal relationship between the antinomies in question. A synthesis which could reunite the conscious and the unconscious, thus making a mediation possible between them and not only attempting to explore the ancient mysteries of the psyche with its death and rebirth cults, but reaching what the mystics and prophets had reached before us: the symbolization of the ego and the totality of the Self. A perfect synthesis.

Here we are talking about a partly real possibility given that the individual autonomously represents the story of humanity and simply by narrating the antiquity of his own soul, he goes back across the mythical phases of humanity where there were, for example, myths and gods talking and showing their numinous presence amongst men. (*Numinosum*: literally means occult, frightening, mysterious, holy, magic, saintly or sacred.)

Only in this *mysterium tremendum* is it possible to reactivate magical forces, or mana, as the ancients had done before us, and guide them back to humanity's current destiny, after having integrated them and harmoniously processed the psyche bringing into consciousness the contents of the *mysterium coniunctionis*. C. G Jung first revealed this in 1955. In realizing this dialectic process and synthesis with its unitary and mythical matrix which has always sat in the *anima mundi* of the collective psyche, modern day humanity will eventually be able to notice the fatal errors and the *perils of the soul* which he is going against. Isolated phenomena of disintegration and psychic dissociation are threatening dangers which mark our era. An era which is now uprooted from the soul, myth, and its sacred pre-history. I have not been able to give a linear continuum (among which there are extracts from my previous book *Il Risveglio dell'Intelligenza* (2010) and my book, *The Awakening of Intelligence* (2010), and I hope that the reader can forgive the diverse content and arguments. I have treated these as key readings which can symbolically reveal ulterior clues to a person's internal search as well as being a kind of psychological synthesis.

Diego Pignatelli
4th March 2010

FOREWORD:

Diego Pignatelli's book *Primordial Psyche: A Reliving of the Soul of Ancestor's – A Jungian and Transpersonal Worldview,* is a provocative journey for anyone interested in Jungian psychology, archetypes, mythology, and how the "heroes journey" may have played a role in the history of the human psyche up to the current date. Pignatelli – a psychology writer with an interest in Jungian and transpersonal psychology – invites the reader to consider his proposed synthesis of a new vision: one that incorporates Jungian archetypes and mythology with transpersonal psychology, eastern philosophies, findings from quantum physics, and even the field of near-death experiences. The central message here is that humans have become dissociated with their psyche (soul, or true nature), and need get back to an awareness of unity with all things (thus healing the split, fragmented, or dissociated psyche, in Jungian terms). For the reader who does not have a background or familiarity with Jungian psychology or mythology, at first glance you may find this book a little challenging to understand.

According to Pignatelli, since the beginning of mankind, myths have emerged in all cultures that attempt to answer questions central to our existence. Namely, these questions are: who are we and what happens to us when we die? What is the true nature of our reality? Where did we come from? What is the true nature of consciousness? Drawing from Jungian concepts which operates from the assumption that we all started as a "unified whole collectively", the author suggests that our psyche has become departmentalized and dissociated as a result of Western post-modernism, which embraces materialism as a "cultural norm".

Essentially, the author suggests that Jung's theory of what he termed the "collective unconscious" (which is hypothesized to consist of various archetypes which have been represented by mythology since our beginning), can be observed in various myths that have played out within all of the world's major religions. These heroes take the form of various figures such as Jesus in Christianity, Buddha in Buddhism, to Eastern India symbols such as Shiva and Shakti (the "alchemic process of kundalini representing the union of the cosmic bride and groom"). According to the author, there is a great divide between our unconscious primitive origins (ie: a "universal" consciousness that we all unconsciously seek to reunite with), and the conscious (ie: our everyday awareness limited by the current materialistic worldview). Pignatelli suggests that from a Jungian perspective, the psyche is torn between the unconscious drive to reunite with a "Universal Mother", and is unconsciously rebelling against the reductionist, materialistic Western paradigm that keeps the conscious/psyche suppressed. The end result, according to the author and the Jungian perspective, is psychopathology, madness, and a killing of the creative, artistic, soul's journey. I believe Nietzsche summarized the author's ideas eloquently when he stated "God is dead!".

Pignatelli does an interesting job of synthesizing Jungian and transpersonal concepts of psychosis, while presenting an alternative interpretation of how to transcend this divided self. In his own words:

> This book presents a positive theory of psychosis through the transcendence of the self. My own theory illustrates psychotic phenomena as an ontogenetic process of evolutionary development in the phylogenesis of human history. I have

developed Jungian theory in search of the individuation process by revendicating the psychotic process as well as introducing it as a reorganization of visionary worldviews in the psyche, rather than a biological model of the brain diagnosed by psychiatric criteria as an endogenous psychosis (personal communication, October 19, 2010).

To begin, the author shares his view on how the hero's journey may have played out in Christian ideology, ultimately concluding that this view has largely served to keep the psyche suppressed as a result of concepts such as "original sin" and/or what we must do to "get to heaven" (ie: moral ideologies with social, cultural, and religious implications that really don't offer "spiritual" growth and unification with "The Great" so-called maker). The author then moves on to provide a historical overview of Eastern traditions that embrace a more holistic ideology based on unity, such as The Tao, Eastern India and Hindu traditions such as Tantra, the concept of kundalini, and so on. The author then compares research in the field of transpersonal psychology, such as Grof's holotropic therapy, with a theory called holographic theory in quantum physics to draw analogies about how these may represent segregated aspects of the psyche which can be observed in psychotic states brought about by modern psychological disorders such as schizophrenia and other psychotic disorders. Pignatelli states:

> I traced back its (meaning the "primordial psych") etiology to the Jungian collective unconscious where such numinous phenomena arise. Shamanic rituals and ancestral cults represented a prototype of the ancestral brain arising in psychosis and borderline schizophrenic disorders. I maintain that the creative individual is mostly important for the balance of humankind given his/her compensatory relationship and archetypes of

meaning and often he/she functions as a Symbol or Hero for a possible return to the *Anima Mundi* or ancient worldview: an equilibrium for mediating good and evil, conscious or unconscious forces or complexes referred to by Jung. In such a context a visionary leads humankind on a heroic journey and functions as a dynamic process or resolution in itself. A healing hero whose faith and destiny represent a great task, thus attempts to bring archetypal symbols to humanity (personal communication, October 19, 2010).

In reading this book, it was interesting to see some of these eastern and western ideologies portrayed through the lens of the author, who embraces a Jungian theoretical background to suggest how and why the "collective consciousness" of Western ideologies based on materialism and reductionism are serving to suppress the psyche. While this may very well be a brilliant hypothesis originally made by Jung, one thought that comes to mind is that the social, historical, and cultural context of how and why these ideas emerged must at least be considered so that we can understand how we evolved into our current sociocultural paradigm.

As an example, it's important to keep in mind that Jung lived during the Victorian era where birth to the new "modern science" was taking place and growing exponentially. During this era, this was quite a move forward, as the church was finally starting to loose its authority. It might also be noted that "bloodletting" was considered a form of treating psychological disorders during this time (thank god the scientific method later proved this wrong), Freud was treating depressed patients with cocaine, and women were considered too weak and feeble to work or attend college, as it was widely believed that this could damage their brains and/or uterus. Furthermore, Darwin's theory of natural selection emerged during this time (although he waited some 20 odd years before publishing it due to fears of contradicting the church's reign). Darwin's half cousin, Galton, also proposed the idea of eugenics, suggesting that those of lower intelligence levels should not be allowed to "pass on their genes" and procreate. Intelligence tests later created by Binet were used to identify what they called "feeble-minded people" in this era (mainly consisting of blacks and other immigrant populations) that served to keep them segregated. Consequently, I was left wondering if one can ever really separate oneself from the larger sociocultural paradigm one is immersed in? This is at least interesting food for thought for the reader to ponder. Could this idea of "unification" then, be another lofty example of a mythology coming to save us from our so-called (unconscious) dismay that many are not even aware of? If this is the case, where would we be without a hero?

Cheryl Fracasso, M. S.

CHAPTER 1:
PRIMORDIAL PSYCHE:

A JUNGIAN VISION OF THE UNCONSCIOUS. THE CREATIVE SOUL AND PSYCHIC DISSOCIATION IN MODERN MAN.

Where can one find the roots of creativity for an alienated society, dissociated and conformed to the habits of the masses; false and hypocritical models in which false consciences are masked?

Are we really so far away from madness or do we not want to accept the madness of others so as not to see it moving around in ourselves? Where does the poet's soul sit if not in the madness of a schizophrenic or a saint alienated by his time and by his collective social uses? If not we know how to respond to important questions such as the desacralization and the secondary personalization of myths that have characterized the era of divine rebirth and which today have almost all disappeared into the secular past of the mechanisation of consciousness, then I believe that we will be dishonest with regard to ourselves.

But creativity is not the daughter of history's secularizing destiny. Creativity is the same madness which floods an individual's Uranian and revolutionary conscience – intelligent and intuitive but also prophetic and visionary: a perennial rebel to the conventional laws of the masses.

Many people do not have a creative soul but have a pure, rational comprehension and by virtue of one of their self-sufficient positions on unconscious and emotive components, govern or submit by projecting their own judgements onto subjects which are more creative.

But at the moment, we are witnessing a hypertrophy of consciousness, unhinged from the context of values and archetypal spiritual canons. As a result, secondary personalization, which the demythologization of symbols and their full energy, are making modern man insensitive to such content. Modern art is also suffering from this collective desacralization. But why not believe that where a community exists, so does the individual? Why not see it as a compensatory relationship?

We are talking about the history of man. A history of the individual which, since the most distant primordial eras, has carried humanity's history with it. By nearing the Jungian vision, we are trying to recuperate the meaning of the soul in the world and in the mythological origin of hero.

Where does the creative soul lie if not with hero? Fight the dragon of the unconscious is the password for a humanity which cannot placate its demonic myths. Myths, which like a collective and heterogenic dispersion, fragmented with complexes and values, take the place of the real myth: the myth of unity.

Humanity needs to rediscover unity, which is apparently fragmented by a collective psychic dissociation. Collective individuation is only possible if we want a real and true process of dialectic synthesis between the ego and the unconscious. Also being part of a process of individuation, the two instances are anyway dissociated in our current era more than at any other time. We end up with a hypertrophic barbarization of the conscience with too many unilateral paths. This is the myth of progress and technology, economy, science and medicine. The myth of materialism is failing in front of our eyes.

Even Christian spirituality is not excluded with its patriarchal, institutionalized dogma. We have given directives to politics unilaterally orientated towards all spheres of specialized interest instead of being one of the many charlatan and manipulative voices of a society corrupted by emotive tensions, temperamentally childish with its men of power. This representative emotive of a dynamic component of the unconscious no longer has a place amongst individuals in a community who have in themselves dissociated structures. By virtue of such a discriminating separation of conscious and unconscious and by virtue of this excessive unilateral behaviour, the dynamic-emotive components are discarded and repressed.

The artist's soul with its romantic impulses is alienated from the collective who notices this unconscious threatening outburst. This happens largely amongst the youths of today. The existential and introvert romantic is excluded from a selective and hypertrophic consciousness. There is no meeting of the Anima and the Animus because of psychic impoverishment. The woman, who should have absolved the function of the ego's psychism, frees herself from the risky job. For a girl, the final objective of a competition or a graduation takes the place of the attractive, projected, idealisation towards the romantic Anima of a boy.

But will false collective values put such a meeting off course? Or will it be our insufficient familiarity with complementary opposites or with the process of alchemic synthesis, whose ancient roots are found in ancient Eastern Indian symbols of the psyche's perfection like the energy of the chakra and kundalini yoga?

Shiva is united with the dancing goddess Shakti, in the Tantric, alchemic process of kundalini – the union of the bride and groom. But I am not here to talk about the subtle physiology of kundalini, the process which joins together the two cosmic

3

spouses, deifying them in the human body which as a result becomes a divine macrocosmic domain.

A yogi's journey is to become conscious of this sacred union between man and woman, god and goddess (maithuna). Modern rational and objective discrimination has dualistically divided these natural processes. That is why the young no longer explore universal spiritual principles of existence and move around in activities which are too concretist and mono-referential. In other words they have learnt to mask their ego-persona keeping themselves far from the unconscious with a behaviour which is too conscious and unilateral.

"Far from the unconscious, far from the mother" is an indubitable order which the young learn to accept in today's society. Nevertheless there are rare individuals who do not follow the order imposed by matriarchal laws and dare to fight "primordial parents", managing on the whole to defeat the dragon. These are the outsiders, the great individuals who belong to the category of heroes.

They are the precursors who move the false disenchanted consciousnesses of the unconscious mother, the anima mundi, the birthplace of myths, gods and legends and with their creative power they re-enchant them. They revolutionalize old paradigms and impose new ones which are far from ordinary. It is clear that this creative twist is seen with suspicion and alarm inside a tradition of old cultural values. This twist causes reactions and collective psychisms - real and proper mass epidemics. A creative individual is drastically expelled from his conservative society with old values and will only be able to return through a re-education of values with pre-existing conservative laws. The relationship of compensation between the Great Individual and his society is avoided, and in the worst cases is compromised by such an unquestionable expulsion. He will only be able to return as a hero or dragon slayer – victorious over the forces of evil. He will then be received with all the honours of the substituted symbol of the old canon.

The myth of Hercules and even Christ provide symbolic examples of the soul's redeemer. Perhaps the only meeting that current humanity has with a hero is in the mythologization of Christ. If this myth disappeared even this last hero or king would give up his crown. But we are so underpowered of the sacred that maybe de-Christianisation is already happening. The Marian symbols are the ritual meeting elements of the Great Mother, who Christians and devotees of the Virgin constantly represent to themselves, and so this means a serene behaviour of the conscious towards the unconscious or Universal Mother. But maybe this last process is mystified in the Christian consciousness, falling again into original sin and fleeing from paradise lost - an ouroboros and an ancestral symbol of the myth. This myth is disconnecting itself from consciousness. The fall of angels and the expulsion of Adam from Eden is only the first sequence of this estrangement from the magical and mythical fabric; an estrangement from this celestial paradise to which everybody aspires to return. Original sin as it is taught to children at church is only the first stage of dissociation and dualism which damages the conscious and unconscious. Paradise has been lost forever.

A child will accept duties prescribed by his/her parents. However there are exceptions to this prescribed transition from child to adult-parent. These are exceptions constituted by the creative individual or hero.

According to Barlach (cited in Neumann, 1970) in the *Origins of Consciousness*: "the creative individual, the hero, must evoke images of the future that need to get out of the night in order to give the world a new and better face"

The production of myth originates from the mythopoetic activity of the unconscious in a creative individual. The founder of the myths works on his creative fantasies and enlarges them in his mythopoetic telling. Since Jung knows that the history of humanity has a collective, mythical origin, whose bases are made of archetypes and mythological representations of the collective unconscious, so each individual possesses in his/her brain a detailed cartography of this multi-layered, super-personal basis.

As a result, the inheritance that original man left us in a primitive time is more than ever alive in us. In the creative dimension it comes alive in the mythical image or in the paleological structure (Arieti, 1974) and is highly undifferentiated in a parataxic way from archaic impressions evoked by schizophrenia. This creates pre-personal imbalances in the forms of pathological or psychotic diagnosis, linked to a maternal ouroboros, as in the case of the most primitive forms of borderline types.

The symbiotic state and fusion of the ego and the world is highly hyper-undifferentiated in a dyadic structure fused with the maternal unconscious. But are we not all victims subjected to the authority of the Great Mother? Those who have body-mind identification and are well-balanced in a compensating integrated structure manage to discriminate the object-world, contrary to the borderline subject who starts projective modes through more or less neurotic defense mechanisms. Between the instability of the ego, strongly accentuated in the borderline individual principally connected to the inconstancy of the emotional object there lights up a strong participation mystique which reveals the sense of magic of things, filling and printing them strongly by hand, where as Jung says, the soul of predecessors sits.

In the creative synthesis these primordial elements play a determining role up to the point that an artist, writer, sculptor, or scientist are full of mythical apperceptions when creative contents, all intuitions, and revolutions are revealed. By narrating the innate mythologem in certain creative structures, man narrates his personal story, humanity's story, dragging it from the depths of his unconscious. As Jung (1960) often showed in the *Psychology and Alchemy, Volume 12*, we are faced with archetypal images:

"The mythologeme is a language that is expressed for images and is charged with mythical image "nouveau enriched" from potentiality of meaning. No language can reach the expressive riches of the mythical image. On the contrary of the mythologeme that is an original language and that it is expressed by metaphors". For the individual soul, society's collective scorn is dissociative estrangement otherwise known as alienation. For a soulless world which wanders through the dispersion of identities regrouped to the moral of great quantity, through mystified identities of false cultural figures where a symbol, the only mediator of the unconscious and meaning, has lost supremacy, even the true experiential unity and mythical tale has lost its value - it has been sent to the meta-narratives which post-modernism drastically refuses to accept. Myth is the universal vision and historical truth of things; it represents the hero's epic journey which in a large measure all of humanity should confront. We will understand that the creative person, the hero, can be found in a great divide setting himself out as the trouble-shooter or "unifying symbol" for man's religious, political, psychological, and philosophical conflicts. Maybe one day man will be able to liberate himself from his dreamy odyssey without dragging his *daimon* behind him.

References

Arieti, S. (1955). *Interpretation of schizophrenia* (1st Ed.). Brunner, New York.

Arieti, S. (1967). *The intrapsychic self: Feeling, cognition and creativity in health and mental illness*. New York: Basic Books.

Arieti, S. (1972). *The will to be human*. New York: Quadrangle Books.

Arieti, S. (1974). *Interpretation of schizophrenia*. (2nd Ed.). New York: Basic Books.

Arieti, S. (1976). *Creativity: The magic synthesis*. New York: Basic Books.

Jung, C. G. (1956). *Symbols of transformation*. Collected Works, vol. 5, Bollingen Series XX. Princeton, NJ: Princeton University Press.

Jung, C. G. (1959). *The archetypes and the collective unconscious.* Collected Works, vol. 9,1. Bollingen Series XX. Princeton, N J: Princeton University Press.

Jung, C. G. (1960). *A review of the complex theory.* Collected Works, vol. 8, Bollingen Series XX. Princeton, NJ: Princeton University Press.

Jung, C. G. *Collected works.* Princeton, NJ: University Press and London: Routledge and Kegan Paul LTD.

Jung, C. G., & Kerényi, C. (1969). *Essays on a science of mythology.* Bollingen Series XXII New York: Pantheon Books, Inc.

Jung C. G. (1969). *Mandala symbolism.* R.F.C. Hull (trans.) vol. 9, Part I, Bollingen Series XX. Princeton, NJ: Princeton University Press.

Mahler, M., On human symbiosis and the vicissitudes of individuation. International Univ. Press New York,1968.

Masterson, J. F. & Rinsley, D. B., "The borderline syndrome: The role of the mother in the genesis and psychic structure of the borderline personality".in Rapprochement:the critical subphase of separation-individuation.Jason Aronson,New York,1980,299-329.

Neumann, E. (1970). *Origins and history of consciousness.* Princeton, NJ: Princeton University Press.

Neumann, E (1972). *The great mother.* Princeton, NJ: Princeton U niversity Press.

Piaget, J. (1951). *The child's conception of the world.* London: Humanity Press.

Shamdasani, S. (Ed.) (2009). *The Red Book.*New York/London: Norton.

Jacobi, J. (1965), Complex/Archetype/Symbol in the Work of C. G. Jung, Princeton University Press, 2nd edition (orig 1959).

Jung, C. G. (1912). *Psychology of the Unconscious* : a study of the transformations and symbolisms of the libido, a contribution to the history of the evolution of thought. trans. Hinkle, B. M. (1916), London: Kegan Paul Trench Trubner. (revised in 1952 as *Symbols of Transformation*, Collected Works Vol.5

AN INDIVIDUAL'S SOUL AND MANKIND'S DESTINY

Even madmen are considered sacred in some traditions and tribes, especially by North American Indians. In modern times there is no respect for a human so there is even less respect for God. The god within, which lives in the poetic soul of the seers, is disconnected from the banal indifference of humans as they try to block answers and ask questions of a philosophical or religious nature.

There is no room for poets, seers or saints. Modern man has emigrated and has thus expelled the god within. Theology is no longer the spokesperson of the ultimate spiritual truth in the same way that science is making the meaning of the sacred in modern man useless in front of the collapse of the illusion of rationalism. It is a rationalism which has disenchanted the universe and the *theos* with a science of dogma in which the mechanistic and Cartesian vision of reality reigns.

Medicine and the morning after pill do all they can to disconnect the *theos* in man, this numinous inexplicable, indescribable dimension which opens onto the divine: the *mysterium magnum*. In some eastern civilizations it is totally normal to accept someone as a divinity, whilst in the west this acceptance of someone who is different and who is a god is taboo. Accepting the god within, the *entheos* is taboo in the eyes of a profane person. Paraphrasing the British philosopher Alan Watts, it is a taboo which forbids the knowledge of what man really is: God in other words (Watts, 1966).

Collective man is the alienation of the individual of the soul just as the individual soul is separate from the collective soul, and in a certain way suffers its non-individuation in the collective flux of masses. In other words, as Jung (1967) believed in the *Undiscovered Self,* the soul of a person not yet individuated is still mixed in with the collective psyche and not yet integrated in a Self which is a super ordinate to consciousness. Is this the current alienation for a soul which lives on this earth: the incapacity to mediate between two worlds or between the ego and the unconscious?

This is a key concept in Jungian literature. But there are other hypotheses for which the ego is alienated from the collective context: either because of the strong heroic tendency of a Promethean impulse in which the ego is forced to struggle against the forces of the collective which attempt to suppress it and therefore re-reading the Jung's and Neumann's description of the hero's journey, or because of the incompatibility with his epoch which is not capable of foretelling any hero-saviour, while he feels forced to carry the weight of his titanic hero struggle from both worlds at the price of redemption for humanity? His destiny in some way comes up against the forces which impersonate the collective.

He feels like a stranger in his own home. Even if this individual has all the cards in order to affirm his ego or not, he is tremendously closed and invaded by impersonal forces which struggle to differentiate themselves from the multiplicity and which prevent god from manifesting himself inside a man. The ego as consciousness chooses in this difficult and tortured but heroic destiny to not be the masses. So he chooses not to confuse himself with the collective soul which most knows how to play very well. The mask of the "persona" is not for him. So this is our hero – solitary and a beginner in front of the multiple masks which populate the collective universe of the human game and destiny. As an undervalued and untrained hero, to being a social, infantile, perfect and capricious mask, this solo man does not accept the compromise which collective fate and society give him. He does not become an effeminate narcissist under the collective dominion of the Great Mother but decides the tribulations of the soul, as long as he does not identify with the collective domain of the unconscious, at the cost of an ego weakened by the imminent attacks of the unconscious.

Thus we are joined to the old phenomenon (considered mad by some) of a civilization now too alienated to recognize itself as a saint. We must therefore conclude that in every mad man, saint or poet there is a god. A god maltreated by the absolute lack of respect and reverence for another being, including ourselves. *Numinosum* is an access conceded to a few. The profane live with innate ignorance. For him, the doors to what is sacred and the *mysterium tremendum* are barred but not for the hero spokesperson of an individual soul. He will be the new clairvoyant in an era made corrupt by a great schizophrenia and cultural hysteria of the masses where the symbolic, revelatory meaning has been almost completely buried by man's collective ignorance and rests in the depth of the unconscious. The place where it is fallen and buried. Uses, customs, and vices are the language with which modern man speaks. Ideologies and mass media manipulation have already constructed the fabric of "reality" by modelling the psyche of the masses. Some individuals who are really equipped with an extraordinary sensitivity cannot find themselves in this short circuit system. The worst regime by which an ego wants to free himself from the limits of this banal collective mediocrity.

There is a demand to transcend the two worlds of consciousness and the unconscious in order to reunite the soul with its collective twin. This vision, this dialectic process can be found in the transcendent function. Only by unveiling the thin alchemy between souls (as in a *coniunctio*) can the king reunite with his queen as Jung says, and humanity on finding its hero again, will avoid his dreadful destiny.

A THEORY OF CHRISTIAN FAITH AND THE MYSTIC'S PROPHETIC SOUL

When a Christian says he is looking for God he is doing nothing but looking for himself in truth, hoping in vain to fill this spiritual abyss in relation to the Highest. Institutionalised religions have to mediate this transversal relationship in the moral principles of the *communitas* and Christian *caritas*.

The Christian God is nothing more than a symbolic substitute for every western Catholic for his ego's deeply rooted condition. This is how we explain that Christ injured on the cross, in the projection and identification with every Christian believer is no more than a re-birth of the internal ego of a culture; a western culture where the mystifying law of hypocrisy under the form of altruism and Christian compassion reigns. The mystic on the other hand not participating in the common feeling of the collective herd, lives with the deeply rooted conviction of having seen God and of being in His presence. He is spiritual in that he "sees" and does not believe. Seeing always comes before believing just as a single person comes before a group of people. God appears to them as a vision. Once Carl Jung was asked if he believed in the existence of a supernatural being. He replied that he did not believe it, he was certain. This is the difference between the believer who answers the collective soul's law of the group and the mystic who has visionary experiences. He has conquered the soul or the treasure, because he has won it in battle whilst the group has no individual soul. The treasure is the trophy, the tablets of law revealed to Moses on Sinai. We can understand how the mystic is the revelator, the bringer of culture and new values. The dissociation of our epoch is the absence of a revealing, prophetic soul and so the collective identity decomposes amongst false values. Only the prophet and the visionary maintain cohesion and prevent the fragmentation of the collective.

The revelator represents a "saviour archetype"; he is destined to keep the collective souls and identity united in a state of *participation mystique*. Here where all the energies and dominant archetypes meet as well as the organizers of the psyche, all inclined to his homeostatic balance and to his full functionality. Thus the archetypes are the models a priori, constituents of the psychic structure and universal heritage of mankind. This primordial unity of the psyche is revealed in myth and religion but also in mythological components which respond to the function of archetypes and primordial images.

It is the well-noted concept of archetypes and the Jungian collective unconscious. Archetypes which open up a dominant function of the ego and the unconscious. But the prophet is the only spirit of the ancestors living amongst men and he is the only guide to whom the great Parousia in the Apocalypse of John belongs and will belong. The Hindus identify the end of Aion/Aeon in the frenzied dance of Shiva - the dissolution of the universe - and according to the ancient Mayan calendar in 2012 we will witness the end of the world. Or its hypothetical rebirth?

Interrupting the various hypotheses of the ends of time we can understand how God or the *imago dei* provides a Christian with a compensatory substitute to life and to the established fear of death. This is why he/she claims so strongly his/her Catholic belonging. In a world which has lost every reference to values, because all other pagan religions animated by the real spirit of the sacred are torn apart by Christianism which has swept away competition with a propaganda strategy of syncretism amongst the faithful through the works of St Paul and then reinforced itself in the figure of St Peter, the Church has become the real religious *auctoritas* of the whole planet. The church such as the Bride of Christ is also one which preserves man and mankind protects them from the numinous eruption of the divine or from the aim of some redeeming messianic prophet. What a Christian is running away from is himself and his faith is a false mechanism to defend himself from numinous forces of the unconscious which he does not know the identity or nature of. One could say that Christian faith is by nature compensatory because it contributes to a self-preserving homeostatic balance. It keeps a strong hold of old values instead of debating them. The Church has distanced man from what is divine.

In the Tantra, the conception of divine is sacredness and the opening up of the cosmic drama in the body and in the consciousness of the meditating yogi. This is at the same time the dissolution and pro-creator of the universal drama of the eternal *hieros gamos*, and in a progressive absorption by consciousness by stages which lead to a unique real actor (or Atman), man contemplates the absolute within his own body which becomes the domain of the Brahman, from the vital breath of the Spirit (*pneuma* and *spiritus*.) This is the *Tat Tvam Asi* of Hinduism: the You are This. Shiva is the cosmic principle of metaphysical, monistic absolutism for Indians and not a simple *imago dei ad imitatio Christi*. This is the reason why the Church believes that Christ was but will never be among us because the priests have already accepted the idea of the historical Christ and not of the young, living Christ which lives at the heart of a soul of the puer of each child. In a child there is not yet the dualistic matrix of original sin. This theory of original sin which has been called the Fall of Angels developed in the self-conscious knowledge of man of the expulsion from his own lost paradise. It is the division of two psychic instances: the conscious and the unconscious and the progressive emancipation of the first on the original unconscious matrix; this process gave life to the selfish conscience with the fatal consequence of the anthropocentrism of the ego.

The fundamental ethic of the Church is based on this distinction but it has the disadvantage of a hypertrophying of consciousness and in a repression of instinctive and emotional dominants by the unconscious soul. To recuperate the two instances in a *coniunctio oppositorum* means to amplify symbolically the two components in the totality of the psyche and so reach the highest grade of symbolic value of the Self through the magic circle of individuation and the process of entelechy. The Church as a conventional institutional model of reference does not accept the idea that there are other anti-conventional models of reference outside its ethical and spiritual jurisdiction. Like, for example astrology, which is ridiculed as a truly primitive superstition. And the faithful who look at Catholicism do so from a merely conventional point of view.

Christ who is distorted by the believer wins over death in that the childish ego takes up life again and holds on tight to one of its human and cultural identities. It is not Christ *mutatis mutandis* because it is not individuation when the ego remains at a standstill about its own inclinations. Only when this dies does change take place and with this the alchemic transformation of the communion wafer into the body of Christ the symbol of the Self (called Selbst or Jungian *rotondum*).

But in the measure in which this is a process of individuation not everyone will realize it and the majority will be disappointed and inflated by their ego which has saved itself once again by full identification with death. This thought may cost me the disagreement of the reader, but I appeal to the reader because he/she is capable of understanding the psychological truth which is hidden behind Christian mystification which ends up being nothing more than an act of propaganda defended over the centuries. Eliminating the competitive spirit of primitive religions as far back as the ancient Dionysian mysteries and Mithra with the cult of the sacrificial bull, Christian religion proposes a salvation and rebirth of the Ego instead of its death which is what happens in the Egyptian cult of Osiris and the mysteries of Isis.

Only when the ego dies does the hero's deification and advent of his rebirth and resurrection take place. The resurrection is a well-narrated Christian mythologem, for instance the absolute redemptory spirit but it is normally manipulated and we can etymologically substitute the word Christ for the word ego: they are one and the same.

It is always the ego which recuperates and not the spirit seeing that the collective as well as monistic Christian materialism is kept alive by the cohesive force of the ego which has a stable group identity and can stay alive because of it. This is why Catholic priests are such firm believers in life. They are not really convinced that consciousness survives after death. Monistic western materialism has repressed death and fears the original serpent – this archaic symbol of the psyche but one which is also the original womb of life. In this same life is hidden the uterus of this mortal uterus which is ready to eat us up and deliver us back to the chthonic roots of mother earth. The hero separates heaven and earth and beats primordial parents. He is the auto-chthonic hero-god but also the prophet born of the double mother - like Moses who was abandoned on the banks of the River Nile. The prophet and his individual soul is the only creative carrier of culture in the direct and immediate relationship with the sacred and is the only one who possesses the eternal revelation. The relationship between the creative individual and the collective is tied to the relationship of compensation. Thanks to the hero, humanity is not lost and does not fall chewed up into the depths of the mother/unconscious/death which barters with life and takes it back like a carcass lost in the waters of the night. The hero takes death and embraces it in the sacrifice of redemption. The hero, just as Christ is fixed to the cross, represents the heroic sacrifice of man and his process of symbolic rebirth. The historical figure of Christ is not that interesting, he is a symbol of totality and it is his sacrifice which captures the modern psyche. But in terms of Christianity a sacrifice only takes place by the death of something egoical since a Christian never reaches totality but only some symbolic substitutes which bring him ever nearer to a mystic perception.

The Christian Great Mother shows herself to be a capricious godmother who has disempowered her older pagan sisters (Mithraism, Orphism, the cults of Isis and Osiris, Tammuz the Babylonian Christ, the cult of Attis and Adonis, Dionysian celebrations, bacchanalia, Jewish esotericism) and all the other mysteries of death and rebirth. The Christian God is a monothematic patron of a religious cult which has disrobed symbols and dressed them up as pale seraphims or cherubs who are reduced to singing like mortally bored altar boys. Only the swirling, Dionysian, playful dance of Shiva can interrupt this since Shiva represents God and the Devil and at the same time his/her *tremendum* appearance. A Christian with his/her dualistic separatist consciousness, orientated through stereotypes of totems and taboos will never be able to accept that Christ and Antichrist are twins and that one of them is at the on high as the son in the holy spirit. Satan is only the shadow that humanity has projected onto his fears which are represented in a psyche's chthonic roots. Christian dualism means the impossibility of seeing god and the devil dancing together in the same paradisiacal pantheon, both of them involved in the same cosmic game of existence. In other words it is the Christian who has separated the beast from man. This we see in the sacrifice of animals, by which man shows he has not the least bit of respect for them. If universal Buddhist compassion was defended and extended to every manifestation of life including animals and inanimate objects, it seems that only a Christian lacks in sensitivity towards inferior creatures. This confirms Schopenhauer's old theory where animals have been catapulted into a hell where we are no more than their demons and persecutors. Man's ego is far from the cross and yet this seems to be the only way to free himself from his pact with immortality. Thus for every Christian there is the promise that compassion keeps narcissistic love for a faith intact; a faith which ends up being the biggest propagandist, religious operation of all time.

References

Jung, C. G. (1952). *Answer to Job*. Contained in Collected Works Vol. 11. Princeton, NJ: Princeton University Press.

Freud, S. 1955 a. **Totem and Tabu**. London: The Hogarth Press and the Institute of Psycho - Analysis, Vol. XIII.

Jung., C. G. (1979). "Aion:Researches into the phenomenology of the self". Collected Works, Vol.9 Part 2. Bollingen

Neumann, E. (1970). *Origins and history of consciousness*. Princeton, NJ: Princeton University Press.

Neumann, E (1972). *The great mother*. Princeton, NJ: Princeton University Press.

Jung, C. G. (1912). *Psychology of the Unconscious* : a study of the transformations and symbolisms of the libido, a contribution to the history of the evolution of thought. trans. Hinkle, B. M. (1916), London: Kegan Paul Trench Trubner. (revised in 1952 as *Symbols of Transformation*, Collected Works Vol.5

CHAPTER II

3.10. AVATAR: DISCIPLE OF THE INVISIBLE

In Hindi ideology an avatar is the descent of the Divine manifested in the incarnation of a god, a guru or a perfected one (*siddha*.) An avatar is the channel which operates this perfect symbiosis with the Divine. The veil of the intimate sanctuary which opens up in the plenitude of the whole being. The interior divinity is the exterior avatar. The concept of an avatar in India is very widespread and is definitely linked to people's consciousness. What is surprising is that an avatar is an incarnated voice of a god who tears off the illusory veils which make the unique master so invisible.

There are many other epithets used to talk about avatars. In the Middle East a mystic describes himself as a disciple of Khezr and sees in him the invisible master of his teachings. In this *mundus imaginalis* of creative ecstasy and imagination, the secret relationship of this divine investiture is in theophany. Theophanies are the archetypal manifestations of angels and the mystic is their channel. The *ta' wil* (revelation) is revealed to the mystic in the intermediate and numinous world.

The concept of an avatar however is still as far away for those of the Middle East as it is close to the Indians. An avatar is not only the archetypal reflection but the same manifestation of the divine revealed in the mystic's consciousness. The divine regulates himself according to his own intimate directives and is mirrored in the human avatar, like a sun's rays. In this rainbow the consciousness must recognize itself as an extension of the divine. The rainbow is a life's process, blurred in places, where at each stage awareness must reflect the god-light Shiva. In Tantrism, this manifestation is called Khecari: the movement from below towards the sky. Khecari is the complete ecstasy or marvel in which a yogi catches the light (a moving reflection of the god Shiva.) Tradition says that this is kundalini, the serpentine, the vibratory movement which unites Shakti with Shiva. In Tantrism, the superior reality is *anuttara* while the preliminary stage of awareness is called *sada-shiva*. In Shivaism, the last level of truth is in the Bhairavic principle of *parameshvara-shiva*. Consciousness goes through degrees of transition: the illusion of limitation or *kala-mala*. Finding the surge again in the self, consciousness joins the divine just as a bird joins its father or mother bird on a higher branch. In these transitional stages of evolution, one's consciousness reflects the numerous rays of supreme beatitude: the ultimate stage of union with the divine.

LILA: THE COSMIC HIDE AND SEEK

The being takes the shape of the deity in a joint game of bi-dimensional archetypes that, in continuous cosmic cycles, tend to merge in the polyvalent, interdependent energies of Shiva and Shakti. The ultimate end of the cosmic process and of its evolution is the re-appropriation, or mystical union, where the two forces crash. Shiva, here metaphorically represented as a blazing meteor, collides against the cosmic triangle (*navayoni*) and enters in the temporal flux of the goddess, overtaking it and conquering Kali's fury. The yoni of the goddess opens up to the Groom like a cosmic corner.

Space and time represent the psychological sheaths symbolized by Kali, the Shakti of the divine. This feminine deity is the attractor of time. She keeps the stronghold on the existences in her temporal weaves.

In Tantric texts and in the hymns (*mangalas*), Kali has the form of a salamander (*candimangala*) so that the tentacles of the goddess take hold of time and keep up the illusion of maya.

Shiva is symbolized by the awakening mystic consciousness; by the divine who beholds his own creature, time, as a potter beholds the lathe. If time is immobile, Shiva is ready to set it in motion, with his dynamic activity as emanator, who unfolds the phenomenic existence, and destroyer of the universe.

Time regenerates itself only through Shiva. The Bride awaits the Groom in order to start again the universal creation.

The psychological time will run its course, in this troubled human existence that is unaware of the light of the divine. This will go on until He will not be awakened to the Goddess, until the consciousness will not wake up from the slumber of maya.

Kali's game of waiting is the same as the wait of psychological time (kalakala) which devours everything. In fact, in Hindu iconography, Kali is the devourer of corpses killed on the battlefield (*kshetra*), while here Shiva is Mahapetra, the Great Cadaver. In this tale, Shiva pretends to be a corpse in order to extinguish Kali's fury, who here has the task of reanimating her husband by reactivating his body. The iconographic representation recalls the symbiotic collaboration between Kali and Shiva.

Shiva, divine light, in this form is light (*prakasha*) which animates thought-time (*vimarsha*). These two elements constitute the play (*lila*), the entire cosmic game of hide and seek. The Yogi sees the deception of maya and contemplates the divine manifestations as lila. He has overcome every dualism (*advaita*), every differentiation (*vikalpa*), and has reached the Great Mantra, the Universal I. This non-conventional reality, the Mantra of Awareness (*Sada-Shiva*) is the first spark of the divine, but it has to assimilate other flames in order to become one whole fire, one energy: this is Shiva.

The degree of Sada Shiva, first stage, wakes up to the whole spectrum of consciousness (*Shakti*). As he visualizes the wheel made of fire of the forces (*Shakti*), the yogi enters the Great Yantra. The yantra is a bi-dimensional figure, engine of the mandala, and, like the navayonis, represents the cosmic triangle, reflection of the divine.The transfiguration where the yogi awakens to the luminous consciousness (*Shiva-Tattva*) reaches the remaining degrees of Shiva, and entering above the temporal flux of space and time, has to unmake it in the light of cosmic awareness (*buddhi*).

In this game of yantras, in this reintegration via mandala where the universe extends endlessly in many shapes, the path of human and sub-human existence is accomplished in every stage of creation. To recognize the game play (*lila*) means to reach over the phenomenic, temporal and extra-temporal manifestations.

It is the task of the yogi to get move away from the sheaths of space and time in order to see again the divine flow.

This human epoch, its history, its tragedy comes from a hidden illusion, the world – the mayic reflex (*vimarsha*) of the deity. Shiva also has to reach out to the meditating one, help him out of samsara, the circle of transmigrations. Shiva has to become man in the last desperate cry. This cry has to vibrate within Shiva (*spanda*) so that this early symptom (*sada-shiva*) may explode in the fire of the awakened consciousness of the great Bhairava (a hypostasis of Shiva).

In this cogitation the thought "wants to be thought," so that all comes from the fire of the consciousness of the ultimate reality (*anuttara*). As blazing, Shiva comes out of the primordial waters, from the first darkness, and awakens to his awareness, to his own light. By activating, the divine re-unites the shaktis who take Shiva toward Kali. Overcoming the Great Time in orgiastic union with the goddess, Shiva finds again his dimension as Great Lord of Time (*Mahakala*).

For it was he (*tat tvat ams*) who was hiding, believing to be all but himself. The games where the I hides form himself to be revealed in his fullness. This may appear as a cosmic tale, but in this is enclosed our whole universe in his last exasperation—human history.

KUNDALINI:
THE REAWAKENING OF THE SERPENT

Kundalini fascinates many westerners because of its esoteric side. However, the pseudo-pathological side of the Kundalini Syndrome should not be underestimated. Many scientists and psychologists are carrying out research in order to decipher the great mystery of the "serpentine soul". However, Stanislav Grof's team takes things one step further. Stanislav Grof has identified a personal crisis of reawakening in this "serpentine power" (Avalon). He defines this as Spiritual Emergency (Grof & Grof, 1989).

Kundalini is a process of reawakening which could take months or years; it is accompanied by symptoms of destabilization of the subject. Nevertheless, the Kundalini Syndrome includes a real transpersonal crisis, and those who study it admit that the state of kundalini is due to a prolonged, intense spiritual exercise such as yoga, or is a result of past experiences and brushes with death. In each case, kundalini acts as a real and personal pseudo-pathological reawakening which, if wrongly diagnosed or badly interpreted, could be confused with the pathology of depressive or borderline psychoses.

The symptoms of kundalini are of a physiological or psychotic order, and one cannot reject the hypothesis of its strong similarity with schizophrenia. However, trying to suppress the source of this crisis could be risky and could lead the patient straight to death. More research is needed, as supported by C. G. Jung, one of the first pioneers to distinguish a self-healing symptom in kundalini in correlation with the process of what he defines as individuation. Research into *mandala* and their psychological meanings induced

Jung to interpret kundalini as a phase or a creative power of reintegration and transfiguration (Jung, 1932).

In Hindu myths, transfiguration is emphasised by the dynamic reawakening of Shiva, the god of the cosmic dance and the groom who, by marrying his bride the goddess Shakti, favours kundalini. The reawakening state happens in phases and by degrees. These are called *chakra*, the points of reawakening situated in the body along the backbone. This is where the power of the serpent lies. This power is latent in each individual but can be reawakened at any time, especially if stimulated by what Jung defines as "figurative, aesthetic images", a drawing of the mandala, for example, where one accesses a superior, transcendent phase.

More than a psychosis, kundalini is a reawakening to the transcendence of the mystic-psycho-spiritual matrix, and transpersonal psychology, contrary to orthodox psychiatry, is not far away. The symptoms of kundalini are of a physiological nature: trembling, tingling sensations, a change in heartbeat, involuntary sudden movements of the body, spasms, cramps, depersonalisation, depression and an altered breathing rate. If someone is affected by kundalini he/she may feel suffocated or can barely manage to breathe. This is the result of "pre-yoga" phases, in other words prolonged breathing exercises (*samadhi*), in which the present karma of the individual has surfaced as psychogenic material and agents. In a clinical framework, kundalini chould be treated with suppressive medicine and anti-depressants. However, as transpersonal researchers have discovered, kundalini is understood as a reawakening phase of spiritual emergency and, if it is not obstructed or blocked in any way, can come speed the process of recovery.

In conclusion, the kundalini syndrome, recently diagnosed by the American Psychiatric Association as a "spiritual and religious problem" (Lukoff, Lu, & Turner, 1998), is a real personal pseudo-pathological enigma. Modern psychiatry finds it hard to solve, since psychiatry lacks the basic theoretical support reqired. This support has existed for centuries in an esoteric, thousand-year old science like the vedanta of the Hindu matrix, or vedic science, which integrates itself into a holistic support in the pseudo-pathological framework of kundalini, stabilising the pranic disturbances of breathing and channelling the energy of the chakras to the source of the serpentine reawakening.

References

Bentov, I. (1990). *Micromotion of the body as a factor in development of the nervous system.* In J. White J. (Ed.).

Greyson, B. (2000). Some neuropsychological correlates of the phisyo-kuṇdalinī syndrome. *Journal of Transpersonal Psychology, 32,*123-134.

Greyson, B. (1993). The physio-kuṇdalinī syndrome and mental illness. *Journal of Transpersonal Psychology, 25*(43), 58.

Grof, S. & Grof, C. (1989). Spiritual emergency: When personal transformation becomes a crisis. In J. P. Tarcher, (Ed.). *New Consciousness Reader.* Los Angeles: J. P. Tarcher.

Grof, S. & Grof, C. (2000). *The Stormy search for the self.* New York: Perigee Tarcher, Los Angeles: (Putnam Publication).

Hansen, G. (1995). Schizophrenia or spiritual crisis? On raising the kundalini and its diagnostic classification. *Weekly Journal of Danish Medical Association.*

Lukoff, D., Lu, F. G., & Turner, R. (1998). From spiritual emergency to spiritual problem: The transpersonal roots of the New DSM-IV category. *Journal of Humanistic Psychology,* 38 (2), 21-50.

Sannella, L. (1975). *Kundalini, psychosis or transcendence?* San Francisco: Dakin.

Scotton, B. W. (1996).The phenomenology and treatment of kuṇdalinī. In B. W. Scotton, A. B. Chinen, & J. R. Battista

(Eds.), *Textbook of transpersonal psychiatry and psychology*, pp. 261-270. New York: Basic Books Inc.

Shamdasani, S. (Ed.) (1996). Jung, C. G. - The psychology of kundalini yoga: Notes of the seminar given in 1932. Princeton, NJ: Princeton University Press.

White, J. (1990). *Kundalini evolution and enlightenment.* New York: Paragon House.

MYTHOLOGEMS:
THE PORTALS OF THE UNCONSCIOUS

Where consciousness and unconscious collaborate we find a synthesis, another reintegrated binominal from these two spheres. The cooperation of the binomial conscious/unconscious opens up new perspectives, portals of sacred and mythological spaces and archetypal mythologems.

This perspective is a widening of a sacred door or sanctuary depicted in the Jungian *rotundum*, the so-called *mandala,* which is a sacred enclosed space for Buddhists and Hindus. Where there is collaboration there is at last an alchemic union, a *coniunctio,* also known as a mystic wedding. The synthesis of an alchemic union is, following Jung's classic description, the complement between *Anima* and *Animus.* While the happening of primordial unconscious or indeed the collective unconscious, agents and autonomous models which govern psychic life, archaic motifs denominated archetypes, their flow in the drama of the psyche represents their invasion of the psychic sphere.

In the unconscious region, we again find mythologems which belong to a primordial layer of collective identity. There is a layer which finds itself in states of amplified perception, magical rituals of primitives, witches and shamans. In this layer the intermediate dimension dwells; bridges between the kingdom of the living and the dead, the forebears of ancestral humanity. Here is the bridge of the gods, with whom the shaman is the spiritual mediator, poured into the sacred enclosed space or mandala. The *coniunctio* in fact shows up in the *rotundum* (the symbol of a numinous experience), it is a mandala with eight petals depicting Shiva Srikantha, directed with his pity in four directions or spatial regions. The mandala is a *mundus*, a centre of psychic totality in which the so-called centre expands until it irradiates. A meditator must proclaim the texts of Mahasuka, an infinity of rays which expand in the four cardinal points of cosmic space. Star Gates are four-part patterns which also lie beneath the sacred doors projected in the four directions of space. A connection with the four cardinal points can be found both in Jung's mandala and in Zimmer's two-dimensional Yantra.

Even the Indian swastika is a symbol which indicates the four cardinal points or the Axis Mundi of the universe. In cosmogonies, mythologems hide from this axis mundi as in the Hindu myth of Brahman, or in the Hindu-Buddhist pillars of Ashoka, the first Indian king who was also the patron and disseminator of Buddhism. The cosmic axis is a mythologem which goes back to the origins of unconscious, to the primeval, mythical and archaic era which revealed the divine struggle between light and darkness. In the Vedic myth, Indra fights and defeats the shadowy forces of complex and broken Vritra, who risks threatening and obscuring the universe in a regressive, primordial and shapeless tendency. From this example, one resorts to the significance of analytical psychology, where unconscious is the broken and dispersive force that risks threatening the myth, or to put it better: the conative tension which takes place with the cosmogonic god Indra. But the same tension is used to resolve opposites which the two regions of consciousness and unconscious flee from the complementary binominal in the process of union and total synthesis. Liberation comes from this harmonious synthesis; liberation from the assertive forces of unconscious which are often destructive. In the mandala this unifying synthesis (called *Selbst* by Jung) takes place. In other words, it is individuation process.

Becoming aware of individuation is a state of transcending the usual limitations of the self. This leads to an inter-planetary, cosmic, compassionate and transpersonal feeling. It wakes consciousness up to the design of entire humanity and a jovial return to life. Here the conscious and unconscious binominal opens up to a cosmic and mythologemic vision and the great mystery of existence.

References

Jung, C. G., & Kerényi, K. (1949). *Essays on a science of mythology.* Bollingen Series XXII. New York: Pantheon Books.

Jung, C. G. (1956). *Symbols of transformation.* Collected Works, vol. 5, Bollingen Series XX. Princeton, NJ: Princeton University Press.

Jung, C. G. (1959). *The archetypes and the collective unconscious.* Collected Works, vol. 9,1. Bollingen Series XX, Princeton, NJ: Princeton University Press.

Jung, C. G. (1960). *A review of the complex theory.* Collected Works, vol. 8, Bollingen Series XX. Princeton, NJ: Princeton University Press.

Zimmer, H., (1946). In J. Campbell (Ed.). *Myths and symbols in Indian art and civilization.* Princeton, NJ: Princeton University Press.

CHAPTER III

A NEW COSMOGONY

What follows is a cosmogonic fable of beginnings. One of my many interpretations. Nothing is proven or documented from a historical or philological point of view. All I ask is that you link it together as a tale, nothing more.

In the beginning there was a nucleus, a matrix of all archetypes and all universes, images and perceptions. It was like a spider – a unique centre in the cosmic spider's web. Just like a huge spider it intertwined its threads projecting and reabsorbing them in a concentric circle (Bhradaranyaka Upanishad). The universe was the loom of its games. But from this nucleus, the universes continued to proliferate. The hiding place of the spider drew consciousness from its archetypes, eidetic images that Jung called Archetypes of the Collective Unconscious.

Then this spider played in the unconscious and wove symbolic and archetypal threads. This spider is the bindu point in Hindu cosmogony. It is the primordial absolute, the nucleus which opens up for cosmic eras and eons releasing the unobvious and expanding the tangible. This spider is the Absolute which radiates energy and dissolves the whole of the circumference of the spider's web. In this zero dimension, energy cannot be contracted or condensed, so it expands. In a pattern of introjections and extroversions, the spider weaves in this cosmic configuration which, like a two-dimensional Yantra (a concentric configuration) expands and retracts. From the centre of the Yantra, the lines of strength irradiate outwards in concentric circles and dissolve the entire external circumference. The heart of this pulse is the magic polarised by the divine, cosmogonic creation.

The spider wove and enriched its threads. But then one day, at the age of dawn, the florid cities of gold hardened, the ancient dynasties fought to usurp its place, and the archetype of the sacred was preserved and then outclassed by a new civilisation. The splendour of Indra's palaces, whose sky reflected the pearly receptacle, moved away from the solid surfaces of disasters eclipsed by the sun. Surya, the sun-god, distanced himself from the ascetics and the clairvoyants. These same ascetics prayed to Indra to free Surya from the cosmic waters which were trapped by the monstrous Vritra (the demon nicknamed Asura) threatened by a total eclipse. Indra freed the sun from the muddle of celestial waters (*svaratih*) and let them flow back thus completing the cosmogonic myth narrated in the Rg Veda. But the civilisations to come darkened and the gods did not last for long. The fluid centre of the cosmos atrophied and a new era came into being, that of Kali yuga.

Kali, the ferocious and jealous goddess of time, killed and substituted the cosmic spider and from her uterus projected a triangular matrix which the whole universe fell victim to. Starving and never satisfied, Kali devoured transmigrating souls. With shears and a necklace of skulls around her neck and at her sides, she waved around in the path of the blood-red lagoon, severing sentient and non-sentient beings' contact with life.

Just as a praying mantis devours her male, Kali danced on the consort Shiva, she sliced the emanating cosmic illusion with her horrifying look.

Kali was the spider and time was a slave to her service. Once Kali had been the belle of three worlds which Shiva had taken a fancy to, even if the gods and demons argued about the young girl because of her beauty. But Kali together with her tendency stood out more because of her ambivalence her beauty.

Kali yuga takes its name from Black Kali and depicts a black apocalyptic age which had regressed with moral and spiritual disorder, where the cosmos no longer breathed from within the temporal coils of the goddess. The gods paled at the sovereign meddling of the goddess of the universe.

The world, the planet of men, is in danger because of environmental, climactic, ecological and spiritual disasters. If everything returns to original Chaos, only re-absorption by Brahman can put an end to Kali's tyranny. Because of entropy we are moving away from galaxies, and like a bubble of perception we will explode in a new big bang. Kali's reign has brought wars, famine and nationalism to people and religions.

It is not over yet because an avatar called Kalki will come down as the last incarnation of Vishnu (the universal patron god of gods) and he will have to fight the tyrannical empress of the universe. The future saviour, the last cosmic avatar, galloping on a baneful white horse will face the demonic Kali. And a new era will begin again, it will be the noeitic era of victory. The era of knowledge of the forces of illusion held in check by an ephemeral sovereign.

TANTRA:
THE MYSTIC OF THE UNIVERSE

The Tantras, sacred verses of Shivaite denomination, stand as a symbol of the universe. An actual mysticism such as Sufism and the Kabballah, the Tantras offer a synthetic and metaphysical outlook of the cosmos. They are the sacred garment where the one materializes in the All and unfolds phonematically in many shapes. Shiva above all is the god who works the synthesis in its five operations of emission, duty, re-absorption, obfuscation and destruction. By sending forth the phonemes, he reabsorbs them in himself and in the plans of consciousness. The superior phonematic syllable sabda-varna (The sounds are the essence of the mantras. All sounds are the essence of Shiva Ishvarapratyabijnahrdaya).

"A" is the vocal from whose unfolding a dualistic distinction between subject and object. "A" is privileged in the sound "AUM" (from A, the Unity, to the multifaceted Aum). Conversely, the reabsorbing (samhara) is from the multifaceted "M" to the One. "A"; for example "MAHA", the process of reiteration and AHam = emission, projection. MAHA symbolizes the ethical order of the universe which returns in itself. The Aham, that is, the I, is the supreme mantra. It is the I the maker of the cosmic process celebrated in Shiva, the paramatman who does not intercede the universe because he rules it as pure consciousness (cit) and as the cosmic matrix from which all forms come into being in categories (*tattvas*), self-reflecting in Shiva's pulsing heart. But consciousness may also contract and take the shape of the multifaceted *idam* in the presence of the divine potencies (*shakti*), who hypnotize the *Aham*. It is the *Aham* who plays the lead in the cosmic scene. Etymologically, Aham is made of the "A" of *anuttara*, which symbolizes the unity-order of the cosmos, the One which transcends the All in the universe before the multifaceted unfolding which culminates in the "M" of "multitude."

It may happen that the aham, the undistinguished consciousness, may be dazzled by the many colours of the Idam, unaware that it is reflecting in one of its projections (*a-suddhi*). Shiva transcends all projections. He is not touched by the dualizing power of illusion and surpasses the duality of the consciousness hypnotised and bathed in the *idam*.

A human being is not very sensitive to ultra-violet light, which has psychedelic characteristics. A psychotic may mistake it for reality, but within both factors lie the hypnotic power of illusion.

Shiva transcends the dyad of time-space in a tri-dimensional triad which has no boundaries. Sambhu's trident, hypostasis of the Lord, represents the dimensions transcended in non-dual unity (*anuttara*), and while the drum (*damaru*) beats, the floating flow of psychological time, the dance rules in the ecstatic initiation of death, reflection of dancing Shiva (*lila-murti*).

It is in this reflection that the person meditating has to visualize how, in a blazing circle, the transcending of the progressive reabsorbing of the plans of consciousness, purified by the fire of the dance of Shiva Nataraja takes place. Shiva stands as a superior Lord of the Wheel (*chakreshvara*) who as a three-headed being fills the universe (Trisiromata, quoted in Ksemaraja, Ishvarapratyabhijnahrdaya). The three-headed being ambiguously is the contracted consciousness (*citta*) who was bathed in the ocean of duality "so as the Blessed has the universe as a body, so its essence in contraption of the consciousness ("citta", Ishvarapratyabijnahrdaya) ".

This ocean is the residence of the Aham, of the superior self, non compressed, but extended as absolute universal consciousness (*cid-atma*). Even the non initiation reaches Shiva if understood as unique principle (*bindu*) in the act of conscience of universal transcendence. The condition of *Shiva-bhattaraka* transcends all and is made of pure light (*prakasha*); to Shiva belong conditions of the being who are only forms of light (*pratyabijnahrdaya*). But there is also a way called "The way of Sambhu," that is Shiva, a way which is purely noetic which sees Shiva as (*turya*), the fourth state, the one that transcends all. Shiva's freedom is in his five operations. It is because of this game (*lila*) that the I-consciousness dares with himself in the attempt to overtake, and the self acknowledges himself as the maker of the Universe-All, of the whole cosmic process and of its origin.

References

Abhinavagupta, P. V. (1999). The secret of tantric mysticism by Jaideva Singh, Swami Lakshmanjee, and Motilal Banarsidass. In R. Gnoli (Ed.). *Luce delle Sacre Scritture*. Milano: Adelphi Edizioni.

Ronconi, P. F. (1987). *Vak la parola primordiale*. Pungitopo, ME: Italy.

ARCHETYPES OF REVELATION

Life keeps going like a piece of thread interwoven with archetypes which are hidden and then uncover themselves in the meshes of an eternal present. Archetypes are part of a flicker of plans and symbols—intuitions which appear in the dynamic debate about time.

The phenomenon of these symbols, or clues, is the same archetypal nature that takes place amongst the workings of the Divine. Their voice seems to belong to a hidden order. By nature, the self that is thought hides and uncovers itself among the archetypes, and among the phenomena of light, shade, sound and silence.

"Freedom of the self consists as much in the differentiation of what is not differentiated, as in unification, with an interior synthesis, of what is differentiated" (cited in Gnoli, 1999, p. 28). This verse from Abhinavagupta, the greatest Indian philosophical thinker who lived in Kashmir in the 10th and 11th centuries, clarifies every sort of speculation about the dynamic nature of light and thought which is expressed and becomes a phenomenon itself by shaping and re-shaping itself in the mirror of the divine.

"The things that we see around us, and with these and our own interior motions, there are no others, say the shaivaite, if not images (*abhasa*), free manifestations of the force of the self which through these, expresses and affirms itself" (cited in Gnoli, 1999, p. 28).

Irradiation is, for the shaivaite, the same nature as Shiva, it is the light of consciousness, the universal source which has always used the self-revealing manifestation of everything in the noumenic and phenomenal existence of its resplendent arch.

This reality is a projection—a playful manifestation, as the Hindus would say, of the god Shiva. Free thought, which through its cosmic use, through its phenomenal differentiation and occultation and its hiding, believing itself to be other than it is, returns to take hold of consciousness, realising the apparent multiplicity of everything and plunging it into the fullness of the self, free from any dualism. But light-thought, the dynamic synthesis of being, is not only a playground for the gods, it is also a revealing downhill slope for archetypes which are actors on the same stage of human life. They act as revelations or as the *mundus imaginalis*, described so thoroughly by Corbin. The revelation of the symbolic light of Shiva is mirrored in the soul, or the *animus*.

"Prakasha-vimarsha is actually the first vibration of light. In this first creative vibration, which ploughs through the quiet sea of consciousness, pre-exists the whole multiplicity (cited in Gnoli, 1999, p. 11)" as Somananda said. Since the freedom of self means differentiating oneself from various others, research or its conation tries hard to resolve the opposites in a *coniunctio oppositorum* of divine reflections. In this conation (which is a synthesis of a perpetual dynamism) the directed way to the divine takes place. The divine is the seat of an undifferentiated link where One becomes many and many becomes One again.

NUMINOUS:
THE ALTAR OF THE SACRED

The plans of ascension are the configuration of that invisible that reveals the sacred nature in numinous. Only when the veil of the numinous is discovered does the sacred show itself in all its plentifullness. Like an altar strewn with incenses and relics, it adorns itself with pulsating magic that is veiling this sacrosanct mystery. The numinous is ecstasy with the divine. The numinous happens through the perception of the invisible, where the world of the invisible opens itself it looms. This perception is the entry amidst the altars of the sacred.

The sufis use the image of the mystic Kabah, the holy black stone, the Hindus use the image of the Ishvara-mantra, the Buddhists that of the mandala, the Taoists use the image of the flying dragons. The urgency of the sacred is a mystical truth for the researchers of the truth.

The mantra is like a mystical syllable that permeates the cosmic universe of the Hindu where the tantras are revealing the arcane. The symbol Shaivaita has emerged in the holy temples of India, at the residence of the cosmic mountain, the centre of the antique worshipping (*kula*) of God and the Goddess (*akula*).

Shiva is the awakening of the supreme enlightenment, the symbol of the consciousness that ultimately has won against illusion, the veiling made by maya. The sacred wants to go out through the door of sanctuary. The ceremonies and the rites of initiation made through baths in ashes are the urgency of the transfigured likeliness of palingenesis, and a revulsion to all levels of consciousness. Shiva is the consciousness that awakens itself through the consciousness in the consciousness where the divine lets the sacred shine.

Sacred like a relic, like a deciphering of the devanagari of sanskrit, sacred like the Ganges.

Sacred like the bull of Shiva, Nandi, sacred like the Goddess Kali with her countless arms, customizing time.

The numinous pulses in the symbol of magical archetypes, of the sacred in all levels of Being, and the supreme ascension, transcends, immanent yet enfolds the numinous. The numinous of the sacred essence shedding like a piece of Indian incense or like the arabesque of a cathedral.

The numinous is like sacred contemplation, like a platonic vision, like the motor of the sky-blue sphere of Aristotle, like the hierarchy of the angels, the cherubs and the celestial intelligences. The Sacred and the pulsating of this numinous is living in God, where time and space ends, and in a single moment in life man can perceive up to a certain point this revealing of the veiled Being in the Being, where all times and all places are flowing into one and unique moment, where his time ends and where the arcane was initiated.

COSMIC WATERS IN THE COSMOGONIC DIMENSION

Water is the cosmogonic dimension in which the self, by involutionary immersion, sinks into the abysses. So, in antithesis to a super-spiritual, evolutionary consideration so well sung about in Rig Veda, we can pass over the myth as a late puranic in the immersion of cosmic waters (*svaratih*), in search of, not in the discovery of, celestial light (*svar*).

Water is the purifying rhythm of life, but immersion in the cosmic balm is divine revelation, it is the seat of immortality. The myth of Indra goes back to immersion, co-agitation and the search for fulfilment through Brahman and supreme prayer. Dhiti, the clairvoyant's vision, is a subterranean immersion of consciousness in the watery and vaporous sub-conscious.

Water is not an ambivalent dimension, but the playground for ambivalences or better still, the base on which the myths fight each other like children of a cosmic night. Clairvoyants used *dhiti* to open up visions, and they penetrated the vaporous tunnels where celestial lights were trapped. If sinking immersion is the first phase, revelation of light is the second, the search which culminates in illumination through a cosmogonic effort in an attempt to free the obstruction which veils the light. The cosmogonic warrior called up by the Rishi, the Veda clairvoyants, is Indra, and light is Indra's reward. Indra is the outer layer who modelled existence from non-existence and created paths through the darkness with the help of the sun.

But the gigantic obstruction, the primordial monster Asura Vrtra, the dark obscurer, pervaded primeval chaos with unknown forces in a primordial universe. Chaos and confusion could not co-exist, so Indra struck Vritra down with his thunderbolt. Vrtra was the chaotic, broken force which held the Sun's hidden energy in the clothes of Surya and Savitr, who were also children of the waters.

And if the Suns hide from the waters, the mystical vision of "dhi" *is* water, a matrix of their creations. From this, water cosmogony takes place and from the search for the divine situated in the abysses of an ancestral sub-conscious, re-emerges in the awareness of celestial light. It almost sounds like a fable, but it is not. Water is the myth of creation by whose powers Indra created the earthly and dual world and led it away from the undifferentiated, broken complex; a regressive cycle which is repeated in the "Creation at the hands of the Wild Boar," in the myth of Vishnu the victor over Ananta, the gigantic serpent which threatened the universe between its coils.

Cosmic waters are at the base of this primordial event. Vishnu, god of life, sleeps above the clairvoyants, caressed by his wife Sri Lakshmi, in the waters which run into a state of suspension (*moha*) between the disappearance of one universe and the birth of another.

Waters also have a purifying nature, like the bathing ritual in the Ganges, the sacred river in which it is said that every Hindu can be reborn into one of Vishnu's paradises, Vaikuntha or as a servant in the domain of Shiva; in other words beside these gods. Offering up a prayer with sanctified water (*argha*) is among the rites of Brahman initiation (*diksha*). The act of immersion and bathing in the Ganges takes up the cosmogonic principle that the cosmic waters are the divine flow of cosmogonic events.

Prayers of adoration with flowers of incense, bathing and linga constitute the Shaivite image of immersion—from immanence to transcendence, from idam to divine ipseity. Ashuddi is dispersion into idam, into multiplicity, while shudda is immersion of the self in awareness, in the heart of Shiva (*Hridaya*).

Between these two operations of Shiva, water is the receptacle of awareness in the state of immersion of the self as a re-appropriation of a cosmogonic dimension. Water is in favour of such a dimension (and is favourable). The Sanskrit characters devanagari were seen as notable in water and from them the meditators and devoted recited mantras, carried out dhiti and visualisations.

Water is a symbol of transformation; it is the border between parallel worlds. The myth of creation tells of a gigantic cosmic egg covered in primordial waters of the universe. The lotus symbolises water's exit from darkness, but it is also a mythical-cosmogonic symbol of the creation of the gods and cosmic centre like mount Meru where devas lived. Brahma, the god of gods who appeared from Vishnu's belly button, sleeps in primordial waters to give life to a new creation. Maintaining the waters in their dispersion and involution puts forward again the course of life and myth. The myth of creation. Water is also a vehicle of descent for the cosmic avatar, as it is the border between the earthly and ultra-earthly world, between the sensitive and super-sensitive world. Water is the kingdom of the amphibious male naga and the nagini female snakes, as well as princesses who live in the deep waters, and the makara, aquatic dragons represented by sculptures on Hindu torana.

The makara is an aquatic monster generated by waters to fight the Sura divinities and to threaten cosmic order (*rita*) which gods like Indra and Agni obey. The makara, to use a more appropriate adjective, are anthropomorphic creatures, once they were devas, celestial divinities, but they became demons (*asura*). Consanguinity links Asura and the gods (*Sura*) and this is repeated in the myth of Veda. A struggle between children of the night and children of light swimming in the bottom of the cosmic abyss where the waters are creation and resurrection, absorption and catharsis, vision and exaltation.

Divine Madness: Unveiling the Myth of Psychosis Reliving of the Ancient Soul of the Ancestors

Does madness exist? I don't think so. In other words we are speaking about the complexity of the human psyche.What people call madness is a gateway to the numinous. Mad people are possessed by gods; they are the repositories of ancient truths and promethean beings that are able to access the numinous as well as to connect with the superpersonal and supernatural forces of the unconscious.

Madness does not really exist except within the narrow medical DSM-IV (APA, 2000) and ICD-9 framework as arbitrary and inadequated categories used as a way of explaining the rich and extraordinary complexity of the human psyche that lies at the threshold of consciousness and is not protected by eruptions of the intense flooding power of unconscious.

The greatest renowed psychologist, C. G. Jung, is believed to have been crazy. Jung was a divine visionary and extraordinary prophet of our age as zeitgeist, the Spirit of the Time (cited in Shamdasani, 2009).

Divine Mad brings light to his culture by functioning as compensatory process to humanity and her lost soul. He is a repository of the ancient knowledge, keeper of the archaic and primordial Soul of our Ancestors that has been ripped apart by Religious Dogmas as well as by monistic scientific paradigms. The ancient Myth of the ancient civilizations who lived in the Anima Mundi has been turned off by the emerging Myth of the Science and of the technology.The Ancient soul that lives in anima mundi, the spirit of ancestors appears as chtonic and residual activation of primal mind appearing in ordinary psychotic phenomena and borderline schizophrenic neuroses. These phenomena are "psychoid" in nature, because they are found at the threshold of consciousness, i.e., in a liminal zone.

The borderline individual is like a hero and Titan, struggling between the two worlds (between the superpersonal forces of the unconscious and, in-between the collective forces that tend to destroy him/her while he cannot work in the two worlds at the same time.

Dogmas have killed "God" and "Eros." Christianity has repressed sex in spite of the unidirectional and ethic consciousness that lead into rationality and *consensus gentium.* Metaphysics is dead!

The Church and its followers have killed metaphysics as well as mythology. Chtonic revivals of the primordial psyche appear in psychosis and psychic illness in today's collective psychoses. There is only one way to save humanity, and that is by his dissociation and its daimons that are threatened by humanity in its contemporary conflicts.

The way is returning back to the Ancient Soul, as well as re-discovering the mystery of the Primal Soul of our Ancestors, by travelling to primordial territories of the unconscious psyche where mythology actually resides. But Divine Crazy is the promethean impulse that can get access to gods—the only creative hero whose divine prophecy can warn humanity in time, and the only one who can bring a new symbolic archetype of meaning to humanity; the one who can help humankind release his present detachment from the unconscious.

Even if the Divine Crazy is alienated from people around him he archetypally represents a spiritually elected hero. The one who can redeem humankind from his psychic and spiritual dissociation.

APPENDIX:

TRANSPERSONAL PHENOMENA: A NEW COMPREHENSIVE MODEL OF THE PSYCHE.

Transpersonal Phenomena: a new comprehensive model of the psyche.

Transpersonal researchers explore in depth these phenomena which are relegated to a clinical framework of psychosis or schizophrenic psychosis. These distinguish them from their Jungian colleagues by the fact that they do see everything as a derivation of the unconscious or collective psychism.

Transpersonal psychologists seem to be more interested in transcendence and everything which transcends the psyche and consciousness. Whilst the Jungians maintain that there can be archetypal visions and mythical images, but without a full real contact with the archetypal object in question, the transpersonal theorists maintain that one can experience these visions effectively on a more than ontological level and explore in them the various dimensions on an even deeper level.

Jungians maintain that consciousness is a derivative of the unconscious (Neumann, 1946, 1956). On the contrary, the transpersonal theorists maintain that consciousness is the main cause of existence like Brahman/Atman of the Hindu religions, and not a simple surrogate of the unconscious or an epiphenomenon of matter (Grof, 1998).

A transpersonal researcher turns more to transcendence, peak experiences and full identification with the cosmos. This is why they talk of cosmic or planetary consciousness or identification with animals, totems, spirit guides, plants, minerals, or even identification in phylogenetic, cosmogenetic, racial, karmic experiences and so on.

In the transpersonal framework it is also possible to have full archetypal identification inside the uterus in the birth canal and to relive such episodes in a mature state through systematic experiential self-exploration of, for example, traumatic birth and perinatal experiences (Grof, 1975, 1985, 1988, 2010).

Amongst the transpersonal experiences which provide an alternative and wide spectrum of understanding in alternative to psychosis that are met in ultra-terrestrial and mythological worlds we find visitations amongst various cultures' symbols, initiation rites, out of body experiences (OBE) and near death experiences (NDE), experiences inside a tunnel with a white light at the end, and explorations of the intermediate dimension of birth in bardo thodol (Evans-Wentz, 1968). Mystical crises, like a creative illness which led Jung to personally experience a psychotic exploration of the unconscious, are integrated in a perfect transpersonal diagnosis as a real shamanic illness. Transpersonal researchers are exponents of these ideas which are silenced with the regressive infantilism of a psyche in the academic mainstream of science which is founded on monistic, materialistic and reductionistic paradigm and does not consider experiences such as the spiritual elevation of the psyche and a transcendence of boundaries of ego and consciousness to be possible. Transpersonal science tries to weaken this Cartesian model with its alternative ad hoc hypotheses which constitute a new vision of everything; it is cutting-edge compared to the old, scientific framework of reference.

Amongst the main figures of transpersonal theory and amongst those who have always tried to attack the Newtonian-Cartesian concept and thus the mechanistic, materialistic vision of reality, we find Stanislav Grof and Ken Wilber as well as anti-skeptical parapsychologist and mythologist Stanley Krippner. We find also Rick Tarnas, professor of the History of Culture and Philosophy at the California Institute of Integral Studies (CIIS) and a profound expert on archetypal astrology (Tarnas, 2006.)

The transpersonal vision is a new perspective, revolutionary force which is still looked upon with diffidence by traditional science but it is gathering consensus by the less orthodox scientific community. One of these theoretical attempts to bridge the gap with more traditionalist science is the brilliant theory of the great systems General Evolution and System Theory scientist: Ervin Laszlo. The ontological foundations of his Akashic psi-field or the store of collective memory do not remind us of Jung's theory of the collective unconscious (Laszlo, 2004, p. 160). Even the holographic model of the brain hypothesized by the famous Stanford neuroscientist Karl Pribram and physicist David Bohm (1971) is held in great respect by transpersonal theorists. To advance theories which are founded on shamanic research, a predecessor of modern studies we find the naturalized American psychiatrist Stanislav Grof with his comprehensive holotropic model of the psyche and also Stanley Krippner who has catalogued and reported statistically on a vast collection or extraordinary clairvoyant, pre-cognitive and healing dreams of shamanic Brazilian tribes. He has also analyzed the dreams of citizens from Argentina, Russia, Japan and America (Krippner & Faith, 2002.) Science, physics, religion, psychology, and philosophy have not seen such a revolution since the time of Galileo or the cataclysmic concept of the old Newtonian movement or the appearance of anti-matter in the first decades of the twentieth century.

Transpersonal visionaries are the precursors of a science which reminds us of the myth and the sacredness of the universe with the determining contribution of Eastern philosophies' great spirituality and from the Tantra's metaphysical derivation. Opting for monistic consciousness, transpersonal psychology takes the psyche and its mystery beyond its true borders. Man who is disenchanted by this sacredness can no longer manage to gather and embrace the numinous manifestation of all these co-creative events which have always been the heritage of ancient civilisations. So it was for our primitive predecessors. Just think that the primitive mind whose revivals live in every day psychoses can, according to transpersonal theorists, be reactivated through psycho-tropic means. These non-specific catalytic agents amplify the consciousness and aid systematic experiential self-exploration of the unconscious (Grof, 1975, 1988.) One of these transpersonal methods of unconscious reactivation is holotropic breathwork: a homeopathic non-pharmacological method created by Grof and his wife Christina (Grof 1975, 1985, 1988, 2000; Grof & Grof, 1989, 2010). This holotropic method welcomes and supports all phenomena which have been called pathological or which have been diagnosed by mainstream psychiatric framework as psychoses or endogenous schizophrenic psychoses. On the contrary, if selectively reactivated by richly visual-experiential or holotropic material constituted by categories of anomalous and perinatal experiences and if understood and even recognized by the new technologies of consciousness (Grof, 1988, 2000), they become important amplifying, transforming and heuristic healing instruments of the psyche. All these phenomena which modern psychiatry relegates to a clinical framework of psychotic disorders or endogenous psychoses (and therefore supposed to be organic but a non-specific nature) are explored on a holotropic level as intrinsic dynamics of the psyche. Therefore tending towards a full and holistic amplification and not towards an identification with one of its particular fragments, constitute parts of the psyche that are returned and integrated into consciousness. The non-ordinary state of consciousness is activated and the powerful, archetypal material emerges and is intensified in the process of hyper-ventilation which, with the help and assistance of the sitter, will support the process until the moment of eventual release of tension and the diminution of archetypal charge which had previously configured the dynamic and complex constellation.

Transitory episodes of a psychotic nature or the most serious psychoses are thus supported by anomalous experiences in which the subject has full identification with the object to explore - whether it is an archetype, a possessive demon, a mythological being, a parapsychological phenomenon, non-ordinary phenomena,kundalini or shamanic energy or elements of an unknown nature. Clearly this experiential identification with the object (which Grof maintains is mystic fusion: Grof, 1975, 1985, 1988, 2000, 2006) could have one of its traditional differential diagnoses in projective identification. But a transpersonal theorist does not put it in these terms.

Retaining that the transpersonal experiences are a legitimate self-manifestation of the psyche but also a transcendence of the normal confines of space, time and random linearity, these experiences refer to an alternative mainstream which fully recognizes the heuristic and transformative potentiality of the psyche by activating the inner healer, who was already fully recognized by ancient and modern shamans. The fact remains that transpersonal psychology defends itself as modern shamanism legitimizing and claiming all these anomalous experiences which have not only an emotional, psycho-somatic or psycho-spiritual orientation but which also embrace a more complete model of transpersonal experiences in their wider spectrum.

Conclusion:

In this synthesis I wanted to delineate a framework of transpersonal psychology by analyzing the differences with Jungian psychology together with its model of therapeutic reference (the analysis of dreams, the mandala and active imagination). For the followers of transpersonal psychology the archetypal phenomena can be widely **experienced** in consciousness and explored instead of being evoked exclusively on an imaginary level as archetypal image-visions.

Assimilating the technologies of consciousness with the aid of indigenous, shamanic therapies and psycho-physical derivations of NOSC (non-ordinary states of consciousness) transpersonal studies make use of an anthropology and in the study of religions, analytical psychology and personal mythology (Feinstein & Krippner, 2006) but as an alternative completes the framework with shamanic research, modern consciousness research including thanatological and parapsychological research and thus bridging the gap between traditional psychology and mysticism, personal and transpersonal, (Grof, 1985, 1988; Ring & Cooper, 2009). This connection is of fundamental importance in the understanding of transpersonal phenomena above all with regard to a holotropic orientation (Grof 1985, 1988, 2000, 2006; Grof & Grof, 1989, 2010).

The experiential systematic studies of Grof & Grof (1989, 2010) underline the healing, heuristic and transformative potential of the psyche through consciousness research (Grof, 1988, 2000). These manifestations which are neglected by modern psychiatry tell us that if these explorations on a regressive, perinatal and holotropic level are adequately understood, borne and recognised, they can be great x-rays of the unconscious. They are capable of favouring a different comprehensive model which opens up to the vast multi-dimensionality of the psyche.

References

Bohm, D. (1987). *Unfolding meaning.* London: Ark

Bohm, D. (1983). *Wholeness and the implicate order.* London: Ark.

Bohm, D. & Peat, F. D. (1987). *Science, order and creativity.* New York: Bantam Books.

Evans,W. W. (1968). *The Tibetan book of the dead.* London: Oxford Universe.

Grof, S. & Grof, C. (2000). *The stormy search for the self.* New York: Perigee Books.

Grof, S. (1975). *Realms of human unconscious: Observations from LSD research.* New York: Viking.

Grof, S. & Grof, C. (1980). *Beyond death.* London: Thames and Hudson.

Grof, S. (1980*).* *LSD psychotherapy.* Pomona, CA: Hunter House.

Grof, S., (1985). Beyond the brain: Birth, death, and transcendence. In *Psychotherapy.* Albany, NY: State University New York Press.

Grof, S. (1988). *The Adventure of Self Discovery.* Albany, NY: State University of New York Press.

Grof, S. (1988). *The Cosmic game: Exploration of the frontiers of human consciousness. Albany.* NY: SUNY Press.

Grof, S. & Grof, C. (1989). Spiritual emergency: When personal transformation becomes a crisis. In J. P. Tarcher (Ed.), *New consciousness reader.* Los Angeles, CA: Tarcher.

Grof, S., Bennett, Z. H. (1992). *The Holotropic mind.* San Francisco, CA: Harper Collins.

Grof, S. (2000). *Psychology of the Future. Lessons from modern consciousness research.* Albany, NY: SUNY Press.

Grof, S. & Grof, C. (2000). *The stormy search for the self.* Los Angeles, CA: Putnam Publications.

Grof, S. & Grof, C. (2010). *Holotropic Breathwork: A new approach to self-exploration and therapy.* Albany, NY: SUNY Press.

Jung, C. G. (1956). *Symbols and transformation.* Collected Works, vol. 5, Bollingen Series XX, Princeton, N J: Princeton University Press.

Jung, C. G. (1959). *The archetypes and the collective unconscious.* Collected Works, vol. 9, 1. Bollingen Series XX, Princeton, NJ: Princeton University Press.

Jung, C. G. (1960). *A review of the complex theory.* Collected Works, vol. 8, Bollingen Series XX. Princeton, NJ: Princeton University Press.

Krippner, S. (1982). Holonomy and parapsychology. In K. Wilber (Ed.). *The holographic paradigm and other paradoxes: Exploring the leading edge of science* (pp. 124-125). Boulder, CO: Shambhala.

Krippner, S. & Faith, (2002). Exotic dreams: A cross-cultural survey. In S. Krippner, Bogzaran, & Carvalho (Eds.), *Extraordinary Dreams* (pp. 73-82). SUNY press.

Krippner, S. & Feinstein, D. (2006). *The mythic path.* Santa Rosa, CA: Energy Psychology Press.

Krippner, S. & Villoldo, A. (1986). *The realms of healing* (3rd Ed.). Berkeley, CA: Celestial Arts

Krippner, S. & Welch, P. (1992). *Spiritual dimensions of healing: From native shamanism to contemporary health care.* New York: Irvington.

Laszlo, E. (1993). *The creative cosmos.* Edinburgh, Scotland: Floris Books.

Laszlo, E. (1995). *The interconnected universe: Conceptual foundations of transdisciplinary unified theory.* London: World Scientific.

Laszlo, E. (2004). *Science and the Akashic field: An integral theory of everything.* Rochester, VT: Inner Traditions.

Lukoff, D., Lu, F., & Turner, R. (1992). Toward a more culturally sensitive DSM-IV: Psychoreligious and psychospiritual problems. *Journal of Nervous and Mental Disease, 180*(11).

McTaggart, L. (2002). *The field: The quest for the secret force of the universe.* New York: Quill/HarperCollins.

Pribram, H. K. (1960). *Plans and the Structure of Behavior.*, Henry Holt & Co.

Pribram, K. H. (1971). *Languages of the brain: Experimental paradoxes and principles in neuropsychology.* New York: Prentice Hall/Brandon House.

Ring, K. & Cooper, S. (1999). *Mindsight: Near-death and out-of-body experiences in the blind* (2nd Ed.). Bloomington, Indiana: iUniverse.

Tarnas, R. (2006). *Cosmos and psyche: Intimations of a new world view.* Penguin Group London/USA (inc)..

Wilber, K. (1977). *The spectrum of consciousness.* Wheaton: Quest.

Wilber K. (1981). *Up from Eden.* New York: Doubleday/Anchor.

Wilber, K. (1982). *A Social God.* New York: Mc Graw-Hill.

Wilber, K. (1982). *The holographic paradigm and other paradoxes.* Boston: Shambhala CO..

Wilber, K. , Engler, J. , Brown, D. P. (1986). *The transformation of consciousness, conventional and contemplative perspective on development.* Boston and London: Shambhala Publications Inc.

Wilber, K. (1980). *The Atman project: A transpersonal view of human development.* Wheaton, Ill. : The Theosophical Publishing House.

Wilber, K. (2000). *A brief history of everything.* Boston: Shambhala Publications.

Wilber, K. (2000). *Integral psychology.* Boston: Shambhala Publications.

THE HOLOGRAPHIC MIND: HOLOGRAPHIC PERCEPTION IN PSYCHOTIC STATES

What I am about to discuss requires careful analysis; intuitive as well as meta-rational analysis.

Let us first focus on the complicated tapestry called consciousness. The universe, the whole Akashic field of the mind (see Laszlo, 1987) is an interconnected network of inte-referential events (see Pribram, 1971).

What consciousness sees as a *unicum,* or a unit, can likewise be glimpsed as a break up or separation. The term schizophrenia means "split or separate". In other words, what mystics perceive as unity, Brahman, or a synthesis of the whole universe, is for a schizophrenic a fragmentation of parts; a division.

Here the holographic process enters into play. Since it has been discovered that the holography of the brain has, like schizophrenia and psychosis, the togetherness of subclasses—a kind of space-time continuum in holographic terms—psychotics live in a universe with a holographic quality. However, instead of being made up of mystical experiences, they also tend to separate things compulsively in a failing auto-compulsive attempt to bring back their "sacred-unity."

According to the theory of the implicate order of Bohm's, psychotics and schizophrenics respond to the implicit category of reality, in other words, they respond to the implicate order. This is an order hidden from view which facilitates the connection with an invisible, sub-quantum universe, a deeper order of existence which underlies the illusion of our daily perception.

The universe is cosmic game, a unified network of events in the multi-dimensional field of consciousness. What mystics see as a unitary field is "Lila" (the Hindu's Cosmic Game). Even a psychotic glimpses this connection but he dissociates it and tends to separate and fragment it. His intention is noble, but the modality of drawing near to the implicate order of things is distorted.

Jung stated that psychotics observe a world which is theirs, rich in primordial images. Their universe has an imaginal quality which Jung calls "numinous." But their access to *numinosum* is transitory and temporary and is subject to intermittent flashes. Psychotics, even if they access the rich material of the unconscious, probably do not manage to integrate it into their consciousness. Thus they are dissociated from the primordial material of the collective unconscious.

This collective layer is the place of gods and pathologies. It is the magic place of the mandala. A mandala is a highly liminal experience which like a hologram reveals a way into a parallel reality. A schizophrenic glimpses this reality, but cannot manage to navigate it, or in other words he cannot manage to move from one field to another without his compulsive selectivity being interrupted and no longer controlled.

Compulsive control is similar to a primitive ritual for driving away occult presences which threaten the psyche's mandala: the enclosure is moved from its sacredness. This attempt at self-preservation is an effort to preserve the sacred enclosure, the throne of divinity. A schizophrenic perceives life interwoven with divine symbols, but he sees fragments since he cannot manage to see the whole thing. The archetypal presence of the mandala is perceived as a dualistic experience. The enclosure becomes a prison.

But holographically speaking, our world is an illusionary bubble of perception. As the transpersonal philosopher Richard Tarnas (2006) suggests, we are no different from schizophrenics with our compulsive tendency to "desacralise." Progress and postmodernity are belittling nature and the cosmos. The mentally ill, as we define them, attempt to restore this cosmos even if they use "primitive" means which are antithetical to consensual reality. Their intention, however, is to sacralise nature, their mind is primitive in the sense that it is mythical. Their perception is primogenious and authentic. Maybe man has one more responsibility when faced with such advanced forms of consciousness and mythical intelligence. An intelligence capable of animating the primordial universe of images, capable of meeting archetypes and mythological motifs of the unconscious.

These structures are primitive in the sense of "archaic" and "liminal." They inhabit "confines"—we call them borderline, paranoid, schizophrenic, psychotic, obsessive and mad; trusting in consensual appearances. However, they are able to permeate the cosmos. What post-modern man has shattered, they put back together, they restore to their sacredness. They perceive the universe as a togetherness of multiple sub-classes. The universe is a "multiplex" to use one of Ken Wilber's (2000) terms. But post-modern culture has downgraded these phenomena by referring to them as anomalies. Is it or is it not an anomaly to desacralise nature and the universe? The myth of progress has shown a gradual decline (Tarnas, 2006). If there is a fault, it is that these anomalies are permeable: they sing of the sound of the cosmos, whilst post-modern man dulls this sound.

We have scarcely evolved enough to talk about it in Jungian terms, but we presume to dominate the evolved forms of the universe. If we observe the hologram and its parts or components, we notice that they are patterns of information about the whole hologram. Even if they are fragmented, these splinters can be re-arranged to make the whole hologram. We live in a cosmic warehouse, but we draw from a single reservoir, from a single reserve of information. To use one of David Bohm's ideas, each tiny, microscopic part of the holographic plate contains the complete image of the super-hologram.

Finally, in the words of Michael Talbot: *"Our brains mathematically construct an objective reality by interpreting frequencies which are basically projections from another dimension, from a deeper order of existence which is beyond space and time."* (Talbot 1991).

References

Laszlo, E. (1987). The psi-field hypothesis. *IS Journal, 4*, 13-28.

Laszlo, E.(1993). *The creative cosmos: A unified science of matter, life, and mind.* Edinburgh: Floris.

Laszlo, E. (1997). *The whispering pond.* New York: Harper Collins.

Laszlo, E. (2001). Human evolution in the third millennium. *Futures*, 1-11.

Laszlo, E. (2004). *Science and the Akashic field: An integral theory of everything.* Rochester, NY: Inner Traditions.

Pribram, K. H. 1971. *Languages of the brain: Experimental paradoxes and principles in neuropsychology.* Englewood Cliffs, N.J.: Prentice-Hall.

Pribram, K. H. (1991). *Brain and perception: Holonomy and structure in figural processing.* Hillsdale, NJ: Lawrence Erlbaum Associates.

Tarnas, R. (2006). *Cosmos and psyche: Intimations of a new world view.* Viking Press, Penguin Group London/USA (inc).

Ullman, M. (1986). Psi and psychopathology. *Society for Psychical Research*,

Wilber, K., *The holographic paradigm.* Boulder, CO: 1982 Shambhala

Wilber, K, J. & Engler, D., Brown, P. (1986). *The Transformation of consciousness, conventional and contemplative perspective on development.* Boston and London: Shambhala.

HERO, SACRIFICE, AND HUMANKIND: A DIFFICULT DIALECTICS.

The dialogue between a creative Hero and Humanity is quite difficult as has always been the case. Jesus Christ was an innovative hero and he was the first bringer of culture but he has charged a price for his own heroic destiny: The Sacrifice. (*Sacrificium* stands for creativity).

Sacrifice stands for creativity as creativity stands for Sacrifice. They go together. Even a schizophrenic borderline hero who suffers on his own alienation from conventional laws at some time is a Titan, representing a Promethean force who struggles against the human common sense in spite of the superior realities and of the symbolic plans in which he strongly believes and obeys.

It is not a negative inflation or something like mana-personality. Only the Heroes are the bringers for culture and these Prophets are constrained to suffering because of the inadequacy of their people and constrained to represent a ZeitGeist among people that do not understand their message. It is a matter of extraordinary that they do respond.

For the hero a normal life must be overcome and surpassed. They obey to an extraordinary life. Human common sense is too poor and belongs to literary minded because of the inadequacy of ordinary people who are incapable to understand Heroes as happened for Jesus Christ who has been rejected from Humankind. Christ was rejected at the charge of his own sacrifice. Sacrifice whose humanity does not want to deal with. So it is up to the hero to take this commitment. Hero, Trickster, Saint, Genius and Prophet represent a breakthrough and cutting- edge revolution in bringing back humankind to its original healing source by symbolically attempting to reconnect humankind with its ancestral root and by representing an archetype of meaning into the darkness of the human mediocrity (see for example Jung and his Zeitgeist CW). The problem is that society and ordinary people have the last word on a heroic destiny. It is not so. As Jungians say, society is always a derivation of the Creative Individual - a Hero.

CONCLUSION

THE PRIMORDIAL PSYCHE

Thanks to the extensive work of C. G. Jung (1907, 1908, 1914) and John Perry (1974, 1976) it is now known that the primordial psyche manifests itself in episodes of a psychotic nature. Material which goes back to the dawn of human history are activated in a psychosis and these are magic-religious.

It is more probable that today's schizophrenia responds to categories with prehistoric, mythical origins from a time when subject and object were still not dualistic states but co-habited in the original *participation mystique;* it is like a reflection of the *anima mundi* of our predecessors.

Historical and proto-historical eras are coming to life again in the psyche of today's psychotic and in the "sympatico" system, which activates "ancient" centres. The reptilian brain reawakens and with it the most ancient mythology, a primordial, anterior nucleus to human consciousness.

We could say that modern man carries bags of experience condensed with all the ancient times since the beginning of evolutive eras. The most ancient form of the ego is the well-known concept of the collective unconscious and the primordial ouroboros and the mythological serpent. If this condensed bag of eschatological experiences and archaic reminiscences is currently dissociated in a modern individual, we cannot therefore say the same about a psychotic person.

Magic-religious influences and ancient superstitions manifest themselves as defence mechanisms of projection and separation, denial and identification in schizophrenic psychoses where a kind of reverence and subjection prevails with the unknown; this is what happens in mythological projection.

A projection which invests with mana the disenchanted world objective which modern man calls real and reanimates with occult presences. The mana power of our ancestors is the mystical, magic-religious formula which prevalently dominates in psychoses; it is the fruit of archaic reminiscences and mnesthic traces.

Psychotic features can be found in the mystics of every time period and this underlines the spiritual and religious matrix of these categories which are arbitrarily diagnosed as anomalous but which are capable of reliving and recreating the worlds of our ancestors in the archaic depths of the psyche.

As the instinctive dynamics invade man, who has conformed to regular society and whose apparent conscious protection is invested with the residue of unconscious material and pulses, so it is with a psychosis whose demarcation line between conscious and unconscious is more permeable so it is impossible to draw a line to discriminate between the two merged zones of the psyche. The borderline psychotic finds himself in a liminal zone between the ego and the unconscious – beyond the threshold of consciousness.

An individual psychotic is invested with archetypal material rather than taking a firm, detached position. Perhaps one other difference between the directed thinking and the fantastic-mythological thinking already discussed by Jung in "Psychology of Unconscious" (1912), is the different behaviour of this latter thing towards the invasion of unconscious material. The power of disenchantment is instead the force of the former which is not invested with instincts and magic influences which simply "happen" in psychotic perception. Not taking any active position, on the influxes of mana, distinguishes the relationship between normal and psychotic perception, the usual dozing off of the unconscious in the indistinct, archaic and primitive mind.

Like primitive man, a psychotic is only the passive spectator of an event which is happening in front of him. The nature of the events is occult and fatal and it is the wish of the gods. The magic of the occult forces and channels of power from the spirit is alive in psychotic delirious perceptions. In the same way, in front of the mana and the power of nature, the primitive mind is clearly wrapped up in mystery and occult, suspended between the sacred and profane and magic-sacral religious rituals.

From this self-protection of the unknown and the mystery which pervades the magic/ancestral universe of our ancestors, we are confronted with religion: this compensatory protection with its exorcisms and its bloody sacrifices. Reverence for the divinity is expressed via rites of mediation in which energy is taken symbolically like *rites d'entrée* and projected towards the occult entity in a magic-religious modality (Jung, 1912.)

We find the same phenomenon again in the obsessive-compulsive neurosis where the energy charge is totally absorbed by compulsive rituals. *Circumambulatio* and primitive rites are the antecedents of today's compulsive disorder. The quota of an all too insufficient libido requires a symbolic possession which thus activates the projection of the symbol towards the consciousness and so acts on the ego.

Only via this possession will energy be able to be mediated and the ego will take its content from it. This happened amongst primitive man which venerated ancient fertility cults to the Mother Goddess – a chthonic symbol of the unconscious psyche. All of this is repeated in psychoses in which the ego weakly tries to mediate and grasp content which all of a sudden overdo it, by way of its psychic weakness. Even if the content shows itself to be violent energetic charges, unfortunately the ego does not manage to take a symbolic hold of the projection of such content and so often it does not enter in to real contact with the content but sees it only in fragments. It is clear that we are in the presence of an archetypal dissociation. This is what Jung refers to as the pathology of the soul.

By virtue of a Jungian therapeutic context which centralises symbols and helps the ego, the consciousness to take the meaning beyond which the symbolic content, only at this moment can modern man relive and immerse himself deeply in the psychotic dimension exploring the unconscious and its archaic demons; he can raise up the ancient powers. Only in this activation of the primordial psyche is it possible to be reunited with the self or symbolically make contact with the deepest dimensions of the soul and interiorise it within the self.

The fundamental role of analytical psychology should be that of putting a mediator between the ego and the unconscious psyche and providing the keys to a deeper meaning of the human dilemma, an archetypal meaning which separates the confines of the ego and the unconscious and which makes a *coniunctio oppositorum* towards the soul and from the soul – therefore towards the Self. This is the meaning which reawakens the energy which clothed the life of the powers evoked by the primal scream of our predecessors. So, in modern man just as in a psychotic there lives a dissociation which at first looks to be more accentuated given the scarce comprehension of meaning and the conflicting tension between the two psychic instances (conscious and unconscious) radically disidentified by the same schemes and cultural rites which characterise pre-industrial civilisations.

The meaning which in ancient times opened a real understanding of unconscious phenomena through shamanic rituals, sacrifices, primitive tribal cults and exorcisms have transformed into pathologies and personality disorders of our times. We have only found a different name and we have given them a differential diagnosis believing we have completely archived them. But we have not managed to placate the cry of the predecessors which they have always claimed to be the soul of the world. It is still man who in historical times had to modify his behaviour with regards to the unconscious. Something that civilised man has stopped doing with the irremediable and fatal consequences of today's world; above all after the advent and the collapse of monistic materialism governed by unconscious dynamics which even elude every control. In other words we have stood by and watched the death of spiritual metaphysics, of spirituality and a dissociation from the ancient to the loss of Christian paternalistic dogma which has split the chthonic rites of religions and the primitive soul with its rites and pagan mysteries, from the ethic-religious codes of Christianity, thus we have buried the true soul of the ancients.

If nothing else, psychosis like schizophrenia, previously called *dementia praecox*, is much closer to the primitive perception of ancient peoples and therefore closer to a reintegrated, individuated journey towards the totality of the apparent psyche. A dimension of the soul which is at the same time a submersion into the ancient world, where the primitive compared himself with his occult presences represented in a hidden, invisible realm: the realm of spirits. These same spirits which cross the threshold of psychosis and invade it with visions which we dare to define as "hallucinatory". Perhaps having one foot in reality and one in the world of spirits has an advantage in psychotic perception. In the psychotic dimension there is the possibility to explore the rich sources of the psyche and its unconscious potentialities unlike the socially adapted individual who does not dare to look at his own demons.

Perhaps the only remains of the archaic psyche which primordial humanity has left in a modern day mind is psychosis. We need to look at it with respect as it is this existential journey of man of antiquity which has always guided him towards radical transformation and self-healing. The ontological process of primitive history becomes quite a real possibility with psychosis. This possibility which we have only just begun to explore is the enormous spectrum of development and personal, human and evolutive growth.

I conclude with one of my observations regarding the current age which has no symbolic, spiritual or archetypal meanings; an age which is far from the primitive psyche and its primordial understanding:

> *"A hero as well as a mystic is given the task of warning mankind of the errors towards which he is moving, and returning him to the vision of the ancients. The hero encourages mankind to pay attention to how far away Western culture has strayed from ancient meaning and from the truth, mysteries and enigmas of life which mankind currently finds inexplicable and irresolvable. Therefore, by moving away from what is presently considered as a "primitive" perception, mankind has actually turned away from the solid basis of mystic reality. Instead, he accepts and embraces a virtual reality which is meaningless."*
>
> *—Diego Pignatelli*

(an extract from D. Pignatelli's Awakening of Intelligence, toward a new psychology of being: Eastern psychologies in the direction of new Transpersonal Theories .iUniverse 2010).

BIOBLIOGRAPHY

Arieti, S., Interpretation of Schizophrenia (1955), First Edition. Translated into several languages. 12 American printings. Brunner, New York.

Arieti, S., The Intrapsychic Self: Feeling, Cognition and Creativity in Health and Mental Illness (1967), Basic Books, New York.

Arieti, S., The Will To Be Human (1972), Quadrangle Books, New York.

Arieti, S., Interpretation of Schizophrenia (1974), Second Edition. Completely revised and expanded. Basic Books, New York.

Arieti, S., Creativity: The Magic Synthesis (1976), Basic Books, New York.

Jung, C. G. 1956. *Symbols of Transformation*. Collected Works, vol. 5, Bollingen Series XX, Princeton, N.J.: Princeton University Press.

———. 1959. *The Archetypes and the Collective Unconscious*. Collected Works, vol. 9,1. Bollingen Series XX, Princeton, N. J.: Princeton University Press.

————. 1960. *A Review of the Complex Theory.* Collected Works, vol. 8, Bollingen Series XX. Princeton: Princeton University Press.

————. 2009. Sonu Shamdasani, ed. *The Red Book.* Norton.

Neumann, Erich. 1972. *The Great Mother.* Princeton, N.J.: Princeton University Press.

Jacobi, J. (1965), Complex/Archetype/Symbol in the Work of C. G. Jung, Princeton University Press, 2nd edition (orig 1959).

Jung, C. G. *Collected Works.* Princeton, N.J.: University Press and London: Routledge and Kegan Paul LTD.

————. 1960. *A Review of the Complex Theory.* Collected Works, vol. 8, Bollingen Series XX. Princeton: Princeton University Press.

Jung, C. G. and C. Kerényi. *Essays on a Science of Mythology.* Bollingen Series XXII New York: Pantheon Books, Inc. .

Jung C. G. 1969. *Mandala Symbolism.* R.F.C. Hull (transl.) vol. 9, Part I, Bollingen Series XX. Princeton, N.J.: Princeton University Press.

Jung, C. G. (1902–1905). *Psychiatric Studies.* **The Collected Works of C. G. Jung** Vol. 1. 1953, ed. Michael Fordham, London: Routledge & Kegan Paul, and Princeton, N.J.: Bollingen. This was the first of 18 volumes plus separate bibliography and index. Not including revisions the set was completed in 1967.

Jung, C. G. (1904–1907) *Studies in Word Association.* London: Routledge & K. Paul. (contained in *Experimental Researches,* Collected Works Vol. 2)

Jung, C. G. (1907). *The Psychology of Dementia Praecox*. (2nd ed. 1936) New York: Nervous and Mental Disease Publ. Co. (contained in <u>*The Psychogenesis of Mental Disease*</u>, Collected Works Vol. 3. This is the disease now known as <u>schizophrenia</u>)

Jung, C. G. (1907–1958). <u>*The Psychogenesis of Mental Disease*</u>. 1991 ed. London: Routledge. (Collected Works Vol. 3)

Jung, C. G. (1912). <u>*Psychology of the Unconscious*</u> : a study of the transformations and symbolisms of the libido, a contribution to the history of the evolution of thought. trans. Hinkle, B. M. (1916), London: Kegan Paul Trench Trubner. (revised in 1952 as <u>*Symbols of Transformation*</u>, Collected Works Vol.5 <u>ISBN 0-691-01815-4</u>)

Jung, C. G., & Long, C. E. (1917). *Collected Papers on Analytical Psychology* (2nd ed.). London: Balliere Tindall & Cox. (contained in <u>*Freud and Psychoanalysis*</u>, Collected Works Vol. 4)

Jung, C. G. (1917, 1928). <u>*Two Essays on Analytical Psychology*</u> (1966 revised 2nd ed. Collected Works Vol. 7). London: Routledge.

Jung, C. G., & Baynes, H. G. (1921). <u>*Psychological Types*</u>, or, *The Psychology of Individuation*. London: Kegan Paul Trench Trubner. (Collected Works Vol.6.

Jung, C. G., Baynes, H. G., & Baynes, C. F. (1928). *Contributions to Analytical Psychology*. London: Routledge & Kegan Paul.

Jung, C. G., & Shamdasani, S. (1932). *The Psychology of Kundalini Yoga*: notes of a seminar by C.G. Jung. 1996 ed. Princeton, N.J.: Princeton University Press.

Jung, C. G. (1933). *Modern Man in Search of a Soul*. London: Kegan Paul Trench Trubner, (1955 ed. Harvest Books.

Jung, C. G., (1934–1954). *The Archetypes and the Collective Unconscious*. (1981 2nd ed. Collected Works Vol.9 Part 1), Princeton, N.J.: Bollingen.

Jung, C. G. (1938). *Psychology and Religion* The Terry Lectures. New Haven: Yale University Press. (contained in *Psychology and Religion: West and East* Collected Works Vol. 11.

Jung, C. G., & Dell, S. M. (1940). *The Integration of the Personality*. London: Routledge and Kegan Paul.

Jung, C. G. (1944). *Psychology and Alchemy* (2nd ed. 1968 Collected Works Vol. 12. London: Routledge.

Jung, C. G. (1947). *Essays on Contemporary Events*. London: Kegan Paul.

Jung, C. G. (1947, revised 1954). *On the Nature of the Psyche*. 1988 ed. London: Ark Paperbacks. (contained in Collected Works Vol. 8)

Jung, C.G. (1949). Foreword, pp. xxi-xxxix (19 pages), to Wilhelm/ Baynes translation of The I Ching or Book of Changes. Bollingen Edition XIX, Princeton University Press.(contained in Collected Works Vol. 11)

Jung, C. G. (1951). *Aion: Researches into the Phenomenology of the Self* (Collected Works Vol. 9 Part 2). Princeton, N.J.: Bollingen.

Jung, C. G. (1952). *Synchronicity: An Acausal Connecting Principle*. 1973 2nd ed. Princeton, N.J.: Princeton University Press. (contained in Collected Works Vol. 8)

Jung, C. G. (1952). *Answer to Job*. 1958 Princeton, N.J.: Princeton University Press (contained in Collected Works Vol. 11)

Jung, C. G. (1956). *Mysterium Coniunctionis: An Inquiry into the Separation and Synthesis of Psychic Opposites in Alchemy*.

London: Routledge. (2nd ed. 1970 Collected Works Vol. 14. This was Jung's last book length work, completed when he was eighty.

Jung, C. G. (1957). *The Undiscovered Self (Present and Future)*. 1959 ed. New York: American Library. 1990 ed. Bollingen (50 p. essay, also contained in collected Works Vol. 10)

Jung, C. G., & De Laszlo, V. S. (1958). *Psyche and Symbol: A Selection from the Writings of C.G. Jung*. Garden City, N.Y.: Doubleday.

Jung, C. G. (1959). *Flying Saucers: A Modern Myth of Things Seen in the Skies*. London: Routledge & Paul, [1959]. 184 p. : illus. ; 19 cm.

Jung, C. G., & De Laszlo, V. S. (1959). *Basic Writings*. New York: Modern Library.

Jung, C. G., & Jaffe A. (1962). *Memories, Dreams, Reflections*. London: Collins. This is Jung's autobiography, recorded and edited by Aniela Jaffe.

Jung, C. G., Evans, R. I., & Jones, E. (1964). *Conversations with Carl Jung and Reactions from Ernest Jones*. New York: Van Nostrand.

Jung, C. G., & Franz, M.-L. v. (1964). *Man and His Symbols*. Garden City, N.Y.: Doubleday.

Jung, C. G. (1966). *The Practice of Psychotherapy: Essays on the Psychology of the Transference and other Subjects* (Collected Works Vol. 16). Princeton, N.J.: Princeton University Press.

Jung, C. G. (1967). *The Development of Personality*. 1991 ed. London: Routledge. Collected Works Vol. 17.

Jung, C. G. (1970). *Four Archetypes; Mother, Rebirth, Spirit, Trickster.* Princeton, N.J.: Princeton University Press. (contained in Collected Works Vol. 9 part 1)

Jung, C. G. (1974). *Dreams.* Princeton, N.J.: Princeton University Press (compilation from Collected Works Vols. 4, 8, 12, 16).

Jung, C. G., & Campbell, J. (1976). *The Portable Jung.* a compilation, New York: Penguin Books.

Jung, C. G., Rothgeb, C. L., Clemens, S. M., & National Clearinghouse for Mental Health Information (U.S.). (1978). *Abstracts of the Collected Works of C.G. Jung.* Washington, D.C.: U.S. Govt. Printing Office.

Jung, C. G., & Antony Storr ed., (1983) *The Essential Jung.* a compilation, Princeton, N.J.: Princeton University Press.

Jung, C. G. (1986). *Psychology and the East.* London: Ark. (contained in Collected Works Vol. 11)

Jung, C. G. (1987). *Dictionary of Analytical Psychology.* London: Ark Paperbacks.

Jung, C. G. (1988). *Psychology and Western Religion.* London: Ark Paperbacks. (contained in Collected Works Vol. 11)

Jung, C. G., Wagner, S., Wagner, G., & Van der Post, L. (1990). *The World Within* C.G. Jung in his own words [videorecording]. New York, NY: Kino International : Dist. by Insight Media.

Jung, C. G., & Hull, R. F. C. (1991). *Psychological Types* (a revised ed.). London: Routlege.

Jung, C. G., & Chodorow, J. (1997). *Jung on Active Imagination.* Princeton, N.J.: Princeton University Press.

Jung, C. G., & Jarrett, J. L. (1998). Jung's *Seminar on Nietzsche's Zarathustra* (Abridged ed.). Princeton, N.J.: Princeton University Press.

Jung, C. G., & Pauli, Wolfgang, C. A. Meier (Editor). (2001). *Atom and Archetype : The Pauli/Jung Letters, 1932-1958*, Princeton, N.J.: Princeton University Press.

Jung, C. G., & Sabini, M. (2002). *The Earth Has a Soul*: the nature writings of C.G. Jung. Berkeley, Calif.: North Atlantic Books.

Jung, C. G., & Victor White. (2007). *The Jung-White Letters*. Philemon Series.

Jung, C. G. (2007). *Children's Dreams*. Philemon Series.

Jung, C. G., & Sonu Shamdasani (Editor). (2009). <u>*The Red Book*</u>. *Liber Novus*, Philemon Series & W.W. Norton & Company.

J. Piaget, The child's conception of the world. London Humanity Press,1951.

ACKNOWLEDGEMENTS

A special thank to generous,supportive and precious persons that helped me to realizing the present project. Two of these in particular are Stanley Krippner and Cheryl Fracasso of the Saybrook University San Francisco USA.

BIBLIOGRAPHY:

Aurobindo. 1964. *On the Veda*. Pondicherry.

Avalon, A. Sir John Woodroffe. 2003 (reprint). *The Serpent Power: The Secrets of Tantric and Shaktic Yoga*. Dover Publications.

Assagioli, R. 1965. *Psychosyntesis: A Manual of Principles and Techniques*. Hobbs, Dorman.

Bentov, I. 1990. *Micromotion of the Body as a Factor in Development of the Nervous System*, in White J edition.

———. 1987. *Unfolding Meaning*. London: Ark.

———. 1983. *Wholeness and the Implicate Order*. London: Ark.

Capra, F. 1982. *The Turning Point: Science, Society, and the Rising Culture*. Simon and Schuster, Bantam.

———. 1975. *The Tao of Physics*.

Combs, A. 2002. *The Radiance of Being: Understanding the Grand Integral Vision; Living the Integral Life* (2nd ed.). St Paul, MN: Paragon House.

Coomaraswamy, A.K. 1943. *Hinduism and Buddhism*. New York: Philosophical Library.

———. 1969. *The Dance of Shiva* New York: The Noonday Press.

Conze, E. 1958, 1975. *Buddhist Wisdom Books*. London: George Allen & Unwin.

Corbin, H.1969, 1998. *Creative Imagination in the Sufism of Ibn 'Arabi*. Princeton, N.J: Princeton University Press. Re-issued in 1998 as *Alone with the Alone*.

Danielou, A. 2002 "Mythes et dieux de l'Inde" Editions du Rocher.

Eliade, M. 1958. *Yoga, Immortality and Freedom*. translated by W. R. Trask. London: Routledge & Kegan Paul.

Ferrer, Jorge.2002. *Revisioning Transpersonal Theory*. Albany, N.Y: State University New York Press.

Filippani, Ronconi P. 1987. *Vak, La Parola Primordiale*. Messina: Ed. Pungitopo.

Freud, S. 1955 a. **Totem and Tabu**. London: The Hogarth Press and the Institute of Psycho - Analysis, Vol. XIII.

Gnoli, R. 1999. "Tantraloka di Abhinavagupta," in *Luce delle Sacre Scritture*. Milano: Adelphi Edizioni.

Teun Goudriaan and Sanjugupta. 1981. *Hindu Tantric and Sakta Literature*. Wiesbaden.

Chamberlain, D. B. 1981. Birth Recall in Hypnosis. *Birth Psychology Bulletin, 2*(2), 14-18.

———.1987. Consciousness at Birth: The Range of Empirical Evidence. In T. R. Verny (ed.), *Pre- and Perinatal Psychology: An Introduction*. 69-90. New York: Human Sciences.

Greyson, B. 1985. A Typology of Near-Death Experiences. *American Journal of Psychiatry*, 142, 967-969.

———.1990. Near-Death Encounters With and Without Near-Death Experiences: Comparative NDE Scale Profiles. *Journal of Near-Death Studies*, 8(3), 151-161.

Grof, S. 1976. *Realms of Human Unconscious*. New York: Viking.

Grof, S. & C. Grof. 1980. *Beyond Death*. London: Thames and Hudson.

Grof, S. 1987. *The Adventure of Self Discovery*. State University of New York Press, Albany NY.

Grof, S. & C. Grof.1989. "Spiritual Emergency: When Personal Transformation becomes a Crisis" (*New Consciousness Reader*). Los Angeles: J. P. Tarcher.

Grof, S. 1975. *Realms of the Human Unconscious: Observations from LSD Research*. New York: Viking Press.

———. 1980. *LSD Psychotherapy*. Pomona, CA: Hunter House.

———. 1985. *Beyond the Brain: Birth, Death, and Transcendence in Psychotherapy*. Albany, N.Y: State University New York Press.

———. 1988. *The Adventure of Self-Discovery*. Albany, N.Y.: State University New York Press

Grof, S. 1998. *The Cosmic Game: Exploration of the Frontiers of Human Consciousness* Albany, N.Y: State University New York Press.

————. 2006. *The Ultimate Journey: Consciousness and the Mystery of Death*. San Francisco: Harper Collins MAPS.

————. 2000. *Psychology of the Future*. Lesson from Modern Consciousness Research.

Grof, S. & C. Grof. 2000. *The Stormy Search of the Self*. New York: Perigee Books. Albany, N.Y: State University New York Press.

Grof, S. 2001. *LSD Psychotherapy*. Florida: MAPS.

————*Realms of the Human Unconscious: Observations from LSD Research* Viking Press, New York, 1975. Paperback: E. P. Dutton, New York, 1976.

————*The Human Encounter with Death*. E. P. Dutton, New York, 1977 (with Joan Halifax).

————*LSD Psychotherapy*. Hunter House, Pomona, California, 1980.

————*Beyond Death: Gates of Consciousness*. Thames & Hudson, London, 1980 (with Christina Grof).

————*Ancient Wisdom and Modern Science*. State University New York (SUNY) Press, Albany, N.Y., 1984 (ed.).

————*Beyond the Brain: Birth, Death, and Transcendence in Psychotherapy*. State University New York (SUNY) Press, Albany, N.Y., 1985.

————*The Adventure of Self-Discovery*. State University New York (SUNY) Press, Albany, N.Y., 1987.

————*Human Survival and Consciousness Evolution.* State University New York (SUNY) Press, Albany, N.Y., 1988 (ed.).

————*Spiritual Emergency: When Personal Transformation Becomes a Crisis.* J. P. Tarcher, Los Angeles, 1989 (ed. with Christina Grof).

————*The Stormy Search for the Self: A Guide to Personal Growth Through Transformational Crises.* Los Angeles: J. P. Tarcher, Los Angeles, 1991 (with Christina Grof).

————*The Holotropic Mind: The Three Levels of Conscious-ness and How They Shape Our Lives.* Harper Collins, San Francisco, CA (with Hal Zina Bennett), 1994.

————*Books of the Dead: Manuals for Living and Dying.* Thames and Hudson, London, 1994.

————*The Cosmic Game: Exploration of the Frontiers of Human Consciousness.* State University New York (SUNY) Press, Albany, N.Y.,1998.

Grof, S. & Grof, C. (2010). *Holotropic Breathwork: A new approach to self-exploration and therapy.* Albany, NY: SUNY

Jacobi, J. (1965), Complex/Archetype/Symbol in the Work of C. G. Jung, Princeton University Press, 2nd edition (orig 1959).

Jung, C. G. 1956. *Symbols of Transformation.* Collected Works, vol. 5, Bollingen Series XX, Princeton, N.J.: Princeton University Press.

————. 1959. *The Archetypes and the Collective Unconscious.* Collected Works, vol. 9,1. Bollingen Series XX, Princeton, N. J.: Princeton University Press.

Jung, C. G. - Shamdasani, S. (Ed.) (1996). The psychology of kundalini yoga: Notes of the seminar given in 1932. Princeton, NJ: Princeton University Press.

————. 1960. *A Review of the Complex Theory*. Collected Works, vol. 8, Bollingen Series XX. Princeton: Princeton University Press.

————. 2009. Sonu Shamdasani, ed. *The Red Book*. Norton New York/England..

Jung, C. G. (1902–1905). *Psychiatric Studies. The Collected Works of C. G. Jung* Vol. 1. 1953, ed. Michael Fordham, London: Routledge & Kegan Paul, and Princeton, N.J.: Bollingen. This was the first of 18 volumes plus separate bibliography and index. Not including revisions the set was completed in 1967.

Jung, C. G. (1904–1907) *Studies in Word Association*. London: Routledge & K. Paul. (contained in *Experimental Researches*, Collected Works Vol. 2)

Jung, C. G. (1907). *The Psychology of Dementia Praecox*. (2nd ed. 1936) New York: Nervous and Mental Disease Publ. Co. (contained in *The Psychogenesis of Mental Disease*, Collected Works Vol. 3. This is the disease now known as schizophrenia)

Jung, C. G. (1907–1958). *The Psychogenesis of Mental Disease*. 1991 ed. London: Routledge. (Collected Works Vol. 3)

Jung, C. G. (1912). *Psychology of the Unconscious* : a study of the transformations and symbolisms of the libido, a contribution to the history of the evolution of thought. trans. Hinkle, B. M. (1916), London: Kegan Paul Trench Trubner. (revised in 1952 as *Symbols of Transformation*, Collected Works Vol.5 ISBN 0-691-01815-4)

Jung, C. G., & Long, C. E. (1917). *Collected Papers on Analytical Psychology* (2nd ed.). London: Balliere Tindall & Cox. (contained in *Freud and Psychoanalysis*, Collected Works Vol. 4)

Jung, C. G. (1917, 1928). *Two Essays on Analytical Psychology* (1966 revised 2nd ed. Collected Works Vol. 7). London: Routledge.

Jung, C. G., & Baynes, H. G. (1921). *Psychological Types*, or, *The Psychology of Individuation*. London: Kegan Paul Trench Trubner. (Collected Works Vol.6.

Jung, C. G., Baynes, H. G., & Baynes, C. F. (1928). *Contributions to Analytical Psychology*. London: Routledge & Kegan Paul.

Jung, C. G., & Shamdasani, S. (1932). *The Psychology of Kundalini Yoga*: notes of a seminar by C.G. Jung. 1996 ed. Princeton, N.J.: Princeton University Press.

Jung, C. G. (1933). *Modern Man in Search of a Soul*. London: Kegan Paul Trench Trubner, (1955 ed. Harvest Books.

Jung, C. G., (1934–1954). *The Archetypes and the Collective Unconscious*. (1981 2nd ed. Collected Works Vol.9 Part 1), Princeton, N.J.: Bollingen.

Jung, C. G. (1938). *Psychology and Religion* The Terry Lectures. New Haven: Yale University Press. (contained in *Psychology and Religion: West and East* Collected Works Vol. 11.

Jung, C. G., & Dell, S. M. (1940). *The Integration of the Personality*. London: Routledge and Kegan Paul.

Jung, C. G. (1944). *Psychology and Alchemy* (2nd ed. 1968 Collected Works Vol. 12 . London: Routledge.

Jung, C. G. (1947). *Essays on Contemporary Events*. London: Kegan Paul.

Jung, C. G. (1947, revised 1954). *On the Nature of the Psyche.* 1988 ed. London: Ark Paperbacks. (contained in Collected Works Vol. 8)

Jung, C.G. (1949). Foreword, pp. xxi-xxxix (19 pages), to Wilhelm/ Baynes translation of The I Ching or Book of Changes. Bollingen Edition XIX, Princeton University Press.(contained in Collected Works Vol. 11)

Jung, C. G. (1951). *Aion: Researches into the Phenomenology of the Self* (Collected Works Vol. 9 Part 2). Princeton, N.J.: Bollingen.

Jung, C. G. (1952). *Synchronicity: An Acausal Connecting Principle.* 1973 2nd ed. Princeton, N.J.: Princeton University Press. (contained in Collected Works Vol. 8)

Jung, C. G. (1952). *Answer to Job.* 1958 Princeton, N.J.: Princeton University Press (contained in Collected Works Vol. 11)

Jung, C. G. (1956). *Mysterium Coniunctionis: An Inquiry into the Separation and Synthesis of Psychic Opposites in Alchemy.* London: Routledge. (2nd ed. 1970 Collected Works Vol. 14. This was Jung's last book length work, completed when he was eighty.

Jung, C. G. (1957). *The Undiscovered Self (Present and Future).* 1959 ed. New York: American Library. 1990 ed. Bollingen (50 p. essay, also contained in collected Works Vol. 10)

Jung, C. G., & De Laszlo, V. S. (1958). *Psyche and Symbol: A Selection from the Writings of C.G. Jung.* Garden City, N.Y.: Doubleday.

Jung, C. G. (1959). *Flying Saucers: A Modern Myth of Things Seen in the Skies.* London: Routledge & Paul, [1959]. 184 p. : illus. ; 19 cm.

Jung, C. G., & De Laszlo, V. S. (1959). *Basic Writings*. New York: Modern Library.

Jung, C. G., & Jaffe A. (1962). *Memories, Dreams, Reflections*. London: Collins. This is Jung's autobiography, recorded and edited by Aniela Jaffe.

Jung, C. G., Evans, R. I., & Jones, E. (1964). *Conversations with Carl Jung and Reactions from Ernest Jones*. New York: Van Nostrand.

Jung, C. G., & Franz, M.-L. v. (1964). *Man and His Symbols*. Garden City, N.Y.: Doubleday.

Jung, C. G. (1966). *The Practice of Psychotherapy: Essays on the Psychology of the Transference and other Subjects* (Collected Works Vol. 16). Princeton, N.J.: Princeton University Press.

Jung, C. G. (1967). *The Development of Personality*. 1991 ed. London: Routledge. Collected Works Vol. 17

Jung, C. G. (1970). *Four Archetypes; Mother, Rebirth, Spirit, Trickster*. Princeton, N.J.: Princeton University Press. (contained in Collected Works Vol. 9 part 1)

Jung, C. G. (1974). *Dreams*. Princeton, N.J.: Princeton University Press (compilation from Collected Works Vols. 4, 8, 12, 16).

Jung, C. G., & Campbell, J. (1976). *The Portable Jung*. a compilation, New York: Penguin Books.

Jung, C. G., Rothgeb, C. L., Clemens, S. M., & National Clearinghouse for Mental Health Information (U.S.). (1978). *Abstracts of the Collected Works of C.G. Jung*. Washington, D.C.: U.S. Govt. Printing Office.

Jung, C. G., & Antony Storr ed., (1983) *The Essential Jung*. a compilation, Princeton, N.J.: Princeton University Press.

Jung, C. G. (1986). *Psychology and the East.* London: Ark. (contained in Collected Works Vol. 11)

Jung, C. G. (1987). *Dictionary of Analytical Psychology.* London: Ark Paperbacks.

Jung, C. G. (1988). *Psychology and Western Religion.* London: Ark Paperbacks. (contained in Collected Works Vol. 11)

Jung, C. G., Wagner, S., Wagner, G., & Van der Post, L. (1990). *The World Within* C.G. Jung in his own words [videorecording]. New York, NY: Kino International : Dist. by Insight Media.

Jung, C. G., & Hull, R. F. C. (1991). *Psychological Types* (a revised ed.). London: Routlege.

Jung, C. G., & Chodorow, J. (1997). *Jung on Active Imagination.* Princeton, N.J.: Princeton University Press.

Jung, C. G., & Jarrett, J. L. (1998). Jung's *Seminar on Nietzsche's Zarathustra* (Abridged ed.). Princeton, N.J.: Princeton University Press.

Jung, C. G., & Pauli, Wolfgang, C. A. Meier (Editor). (2001). *Atom and Archetype : The Pauli/Jung Letters, 1932-1958,* Princeton, N.J.: Princeton University Press.

Jung, C. G., & Sabini, M. (2002). *The Earth Has a Soul*: the nature writings of C.G. Jung. Berkeley, Calif.: North Atlantic Books.

Jung, C. G., & Victor White. (2007). *The Jung-White Letters.* Philemon Series.

Jung, C. G. (2007). *Children's Dreams.* Philemon Series.

Jung, C. G., & Sonu Shamdasani (Editor). (2009).

Aion: Researches into the Phenomenology of the Self (Collected Works of C.G. Jung Vol.9 Part 2) [Paperback]

Jung, C. G.,Volume 12: Psychology and Alchemy (Bollingen Series)

Neumann, Erich. 1972. *The Great Mother.* Princeton, N.J.: Princeton University Press.

Moody, R. A. & P. Perry. 1988. *The Light Beyond.* New York: Bantam.

Jung, C. G., & Sonu Shamdasani (Editor). (2009). <u>*The Red Book.* Liber Novus</u>, Philemon Series & W.W. Norton & Co.

J. Piaget, The child's conception of the world. London Humanity Press,1951.

Krippner, S. 1989. Some touchstones for parapsychological research. In G. K. Zollschan, J. F. Schumaker, & G. F. Walsh (eds.), *Exploring the paranormal: Perspectives on belief and experience* (167-183). Lindfield, New South Wales, Australia: Unity Press.

———. 1990. Frontiers in dreamwork. In S. Krippner (ed.), *Dreamtime and dreamwork: Decoding the language of the night* (207-213). Los Angeles: Tarcher.

———. 1993. Telepathy and dreaming. In M.A. Carskadon (ed.), *Encyclopedia of sleep and dreaming* (612-613). New York: Macmillan.

———. 1994. Waking life, dream life, and the construction of reality. *Anthropology of Consciousness, 5*(3), 17-24.

Krippner, S. & Welch, P. 1992. *Spiritual dimensions of healing: From native shamanism to contemporary health care.* New York: Irvington.

Krippner, S., & J. Dillard. 1988. *Dreamworking.* Buffalo, NY: Bearly.

Krippner, S., M. Ullman & M. Honorton. 1971. A precognitive dream study with a single subject. *Journal of the American Society for Psychical Research,* 65, 192-203.

Krippner, S. & A. Villoldo. 1986. *The realms of healing* (3rd ed.). Berkeley, CA: Celestial Arts

Krippner, S. 1989. Mythological aspects of death and dying. In A. Berger et al. (eds.), *Perspectives on death and dying* (3-13). Philadelphia: Charles Press.

————. 1990. Tribal shamans and their travels into dreamtime. In S. Krippner (ed.), *Dreamtime and dreamwork: Decoding the language of the night* (185-193). Los Angeles: Jeremy P. Tarcher/Perigee.

Krippner, S. & Faith, L. 2001. Exotic dreams: A cross-cultural study. *Dreaming, 11,* 73-82.

Laszlo, E. 1987. The psi-field hypothesis. *IS Journal, 4,* 13-28.

————. 1993. *The creative cosmos: A unified science of matter, life, and mind.* Edinburgh: Floris.

————. 1997. *The whispering pond.* New York: Harper Collins.

————. 2001, Sept. 1. Human evolution in the third millennium. *Futures,* 1-11.

————. 2004. *Science and the Akashic field: An integral theory of everything.* Rochester, NY: Inner Traditions.

Perry, J.,The far side of madness, Prentice-Hall Englewood Cliffs 1974.

Perry, J., Roots and Renewal in Myths and Madness, Jossey-Bass Publ., San Francisco 1976.

Pribram, K. H. 1971. *Languages of the brain: Experimental paradoxes and principles in neuropsychology.* Englewood Cliffs, NJ: Prentice-Hall/Brandon House.

————.1991. *Brain and perception: Holonomy and structure in figural processing.* Hillsdale, NJ: Lawrence Erlbaum Associates.

Pribram, H. K. (1960). *Plans and the Structure of Behavior.*, Henry Holt & Co.

Mahler, M., On human symbiosis and the vicissitudes of individuation. International Univ. Press New York,1968.

Masterson, J. F. & Rinsley, D. B., "The borderline syndrome: The role of the mother in the genesis and psychic structure of the borderline personality".in Rapprochement:the critical subphase of separation-individuation.Jason Aronson,New York,1980,299-329.

Ring K. 1980. *Life at death: Scientific investigation of the near-death experience.* New York: Coward, McCann & Geoghegan.

————. 1984. *Heading toward Omega: Insearch of the meaning of the near-death experience.* New York: William Morrow.

Ring, K. & M. Lawrence, M. 1993. Further evidence for veridical perception during near-death experiences. *Journal of Near-Death Studies, 11*, 223-230.

Talbot, M. 1991. *The Holographic Universe.*

————. 1988. *Beyond the Quantum.* New York: Bantam Books.

Wade, J. 1996. *Changes of mind: A holonomic theory of the evolution of consciousness.* Albany: State University of New York Press.

Wolf, Alan F. *The Dreaming Universe: Investigations of the Middle Realm of Consciousness and Matter* (New York: Summit Books, 1993).

Greyson, B. 1993. The Physio-kuṇḍalinī syndrome and mental illness. *Journal of Transpersonal Psychology*, 25,43,58, Psyc Info Abstract, Accession Number.

————. 2000. Some Neuropsychological correlates of the phisyo-kuṇḍalinī syndrome. *Journal of Transpersonal Psychology*, 32,123-134, PsycInfo Abstract.

Grof, S. *Realms of Human Unconscious*, New York: Viking, 1975.

Grof, S. & C. Grof. 1980. *Beyond Death*. London: Thames and Hudson.

Grof, S. 1988. *The Adventure of Self Discovery*. Albany, NY: State University of New York Press.

Grof, S. & C. Grof. 1989. *Spiritual Emergency: When Personal Transformation becomes a Crisis (New Consciousness Reader)*, Los Angeles, J.P. Tarcher.

Grof, S., H. Zina Bennett. 1992. *The Holotropic mind*. San Francisco: Harper Collins MAPS.

Grof, S. 1998. *The Cosmic Game: Exploration of the Frontiers of Human Consciousness*. Albany, NY: State University of New York Press.

Grof, S. 2006. *The Ultimate Journey: Consciousness and the Mystery of Death*. MAPS ,Florida.

———. 2000. *Psychology of the Future. Lesson from modern consciousness research.* Albany, NY: State University of New York Press.

Grof, S. & Grof C. 2000. *The Stormy Search for the Self.* New York Perigee/Tarcher Los Angeles, CA. Putnam Publications.

Hansen, G. 1995. Schizophrenia or Spiritual Crisis? "On Raising the Kuṇdalini" and its diagnostic classification, *Weekly Journal of Danish Medical Association.*

Hillman, J. 1985. *Anima, an anatomy of personified notion.* Princeton, N.J.: Princeton University Press & London: Routledge and Kegan Paul LTD.

Hillman, J. 1964, 1967. *Betrayal: Senex and Puer.*

James W. 1902. (first ed.), *The varieties of religious experience: A study in human nature.* New York: The modern library, Original edition 1902. New York and London: Longmans Green and Company.

Jung, C. G. *Collected Works.* Princeton, N.J.: University Press and London: Routledge and Kegan Paul LTD.

———. 1960. *A Review of the Complex Theory.* Collected Works, vol. 8, Bollingen Series XX. Princeton: Princeton University Press.

Jung, C. G. and C. Kerényi. *Essays on a Science of Mythology.* Bollingen Series XXII New York: Pantheon Books, Inc. .

Jung C. G. 1969. *Mandala Symbolism.* R.F.C. Hull (transl.) vol. 9, Part I, Bollingen Series XX. Princeton, N.J.: Princeton University Press.

Krippner, S. 1989. Some touchstones for parapsychological research. In G. K. Zollschan, J. F. Schumaker, & G.F. Walsh (eds.), *Exploring the paranormal: Perspectives on belief and experience* (pp. 167-183). Lindfield, New South Wales, Australia: Unity Press.

———. 1990. Frontiers in dreamwork. In S. Krippner (ed.), *Dreamtime and dreamwork: Decoding the language of the night* (pp. 207-213). Los Angeles: Tarcher.

———. 1993. Telepathy and dreaming. In M. A. Carskadon (ed.), *Encyclopedia of sleep and dreaming* (pp. 612-613). New York: Macmillan.

———. 1994. Waking life, dream life, and the construction of reality. *Anthropology of Consciousness,*5(3), 17-24.

Krippner, S. & Dillard, J. 1988. *Dreamworking.* Buffalo, NY: Bearly.

Krippner, S., Ullman, M., & Honorton, M. 1971. A precognitive dream study with a single subject. *Journal of the American Society for Psychical Research, 65,* 192-203.

Krippner, S. & Villoldo, A. 1986. *The realms of healing* (3rd ed.). Berkeley, CA: Celestial Arts

Krippner, S., & Welch, P. 1992. *Spiritual dimensions of healing: From native shamanism to contemporary health care.* New York: Irvington.

Krippner., S., Feinstein D.,The Mythic Path (3 edition) Energy Psychology press Santa Rosa CA 2006.

Lukoff, David, Lu, Francis G., Turner, R. 1998. *From Spiritual Emergency to Spiritual Problem: the Transpersonal roots of the New D-S-M-IV Category,* Journal of Humanistic Psychology, 38 (2),21-50.

Maslow, A. 1962-68. *Toward a Psychology of Being.* London and New York: Van Nostranand Reinhold Co.

Miller, J. 1972. *The Vedas "Harmony, Meditation and Fulfilment,"* Rider and Company London 1974.

Neumann, E. 1970. *Origins and History of Consciousness.* Princeton, N.J.: Princeton University Press.

———. 1972. *The Great Mother.* Princeton, N.J.: Princeton University Press.

Pribram, K. H. 1970. "Feelings as monitors." In M. B. Arnold *Feelings and Emotions.* New York: Academic Press.

Sannella, Lee. 1975. *Kundalini, psychosis or transcendence?* San Francisco: Dakin.

Scotton, Bruce, and Battista (eds.). 1996. *The phenomenology and treatment of kuṇḍalinī,* in "Chinen, Textbook of Transpersonal Psychiatry and Psychology." New York: Basic Books Inc. PsycInfo Abstract.

Singh, J., Lakshmanjee J. 1988. *Abhinavagupta, Parātrīśikā vivarana, the Secret of Tantric Mysticism,* Sri Jainendra press, Motilal Banarsidass, Delhi.

Talbot M. 1991. *The Holographic Universe Copyright Michael Talbot.*

———. 1998. *Beyond the quantum.* New York: Bantam.

Tarnas, R. 2006. *Cosmos and Psyche: Intimations of a New World View.* Viking Penguin.

Tarnas R., *The Passion of the Western mind:understanding the idea that have shaped our world view.* New York Ballantine Books.

G.Tucci, *Induismo,* "Hinduism." ISMEO Roma.

Von Glasenapp, H. 1949. Philosophie der Inder. Alfred Verlag Stuttgart.

Watts, A.W. 1966. *The Book: On the Taboo Against Knowing Who You Are*. New York: Pantheon.

———. 1975. *Tao: The Watercourse Way*. New York: Pantheon.

———. 1983. *Way of Liberation*. ed. Mark Watts. New York: Weatherhill.

———. *Talking Zen*. New York and Tokyo: Weatherhill.

———. 1957. *The Way of Zen*. Pantheon.

White, J. 1990. *Kuṇḍalinī Evolution and Enlightenment*. Paragon House: New York.

Wilber, K. 1977. *The Spectrum of Consciousness*. Wheaton, Ill.: Quest.

———. 1981. *Up from Eden*. New York: Doubleday/Anchor.

———. 1982. *A Social God*. New York McGraw-Hill.

Wilber K. *The Atman project: A transpersonal view of human development*. Wheaton, Ill.: The Theosophical Publishing House 1980.

———. 1982. *The Holographic Paradigm and Other Paradoxes*. Boston: Shambhala, Boston.

Wilber, K., Engler, J., Brown, D.P. 1986. *Transformation of Consciousness: conventional and contemplative perspectives on development*. Boston and London: Shambhala.

———. 2000. *A Brief History of Everything*. Shambhala.

———. 2000. *Integral Psychology*. Shambhala.

Williams, Paul, with Anthony Tribe. 2000. *Buddhist Thought: A Complete Introduction to the Indian Tradition*. London.

Wolf, Alan F. 1993. *The Dreaming Universe: Investigations of the Middle Realm of Consciousness and Matter*. Summit Books: New York.

―――. The Quantum Pshysics of Consciousness: Towards a New Psychology, "Integrative Psychology," Vol. 3 (1985), pp. 236-47; On the Quantum Physical Theory of Subjective Antedating, "Journal of Theoretical Biology," Vol. 136 (1989), 13-19.

―――. 1981. *Taking the Quantum Leap: The New Physics for Nonscientists*, ed. riv. San Francisco: Harper & Row.

Zimmer, H., edited by Campbell J. 1946. *Myths and Symbols in Indian Art and Civilization*. Bollingen Foundation Washington D.C., Princeton University Press, Princeton, N.J.

D. Pignatelli.,The Awakening of Intelligence:Toward a new psychology of being:eastern psychologies in the direction of new Transpersonal Theories.,iUniverse 2010. Foreword by Stanley Krippner Ph.D.

D. Pignatelli., Psiche Primordiale:il misterioso richiamo dell'Anima degli Antenati:visioni transpersonali e mitiche sul mondo (&MyBook 2010) published in Italy.

D. Pignatelli., Il Risveglio dell'Intelligenza:verso una nuova psicologia dell'essere Montedit 2007 –reviewed in the Journal of Transpersonal Psychology Vol. 40 n 1. Book reprinted in &MyBook 2010 Italy

ADDITIONAL BIBLIOGRAPHY:

- Grof S. & Grof C. , Beyond Death, Thames and Hudson, London, 1980

-Grof S. , The Adventure of Self Discovery, State University of New York Press, Albany NY, 1988

-Grof S. & Grof C. , Spiritual Emergency: When Personal Transformation becomes a Crisis (New Consciousness Reader), Los Angeles, J. P. Tarcher, 1989

-Grof, S. 1975. Realms of the Human Unconscious: Observations from LSD Research. New York: Viking Press.

-Grof, S. 1980. LSD Psychotherapy. Pomona, CA: Hunter House.

-Grof S. & Grof C. Holotropic Breathwork: A New Approach to Self-Exploration and Therapy., SUNY 2010.

-Grof, S. 1985. Beyond the Brain: Birth, Death, and Transcendence in Psychotherapy. Albany, N. Y: State University New York Press.

-Grof, S. 1988. The Adventure of Self-Discovery. Albany, N.Y.StateUniversity New York Press.

-Grof S. , Zina Bennett H. , Holotropic mind, Harper Collins MAPS, San Francisco, 1992.

-Grof S. , The Cosmic Game: Exploration of the Frontiers of Human Consciousness, SUNY Press, Albany (New York), 1998.

-Grof S. , Psychology of the Future. Lesson from Modern Consciousness Research, by Stanislav Grof, SUNY Press, Albany (New York), 2000 .

-Grof S. & Grof C. , The Stormy Search for the Self, New York Perigee/ Tarcher Los Angeles, Ca Putnam Publications 2000

-Jung, C. G. 1956. Symbols and Transformation. Collected Works, vol. 5, Bollingen Series XX, Princeton, N. J. : Princeton University Press.

-Jung, C. G. 1959. The Archetypes and the Collective Unconscious. Collected Works, vol. 9, 1. Bollingen Series XX, Princeton, N. J. : Princeton University Press.

-Jung, C. G. 1960. A Review of the Complex Theory. Collected Works, vol. 8, Bollingen Series XX. Princeton: Princeton University Press.

-Krippner, S., & Villoldo, A. (1986). The realms of healing (3rd ed.). Berkeley, CA: Celestial Arts

-Krippner, S., & Welch, P. (1992). Spiritual dimensions of healing: From native shamanism to contemporary health care. New York: Irvington.

-Krippner, S. & Feinstein D. The Mythic Path, Energy Psychology Press 2006 Santa Rosa CA.

-Lukoff, D., Lu, F., Turner, R. (1992). Toward a more culturally sensitive DSM-IV: Psychoreligious and psychospiritual problems. Journal of Nervous and Mental Disease, 180(11),

-Bohm D. , Unfolding meaning, Ark, London, 1987.

-Bohm D. , Wholeness and the implicate order, Ark, London, 1983.

-Bohm D. e Peat F. D. , Science, order and creativity, Bantam Books, New York, 1987

- Krippner & Faith, : Exotic dreams: A cross-cultural survay, Dreaming 11-2001, p.73, 82 in Extraordinary Dreams., Krippner, Bogzaran, Carvalho SUNY press 2002)

-Krippner, S. (1982). Holonomy and parapsychology. In K. Wilber (Ed.), The holographic paradigm and other paradoxes: Exploring the leading edge of science (pp. 124-125). Boulder, CO: Shambhala.

-Laszlo, E. (1993). The creative cosmos. Edinburgh, Scotland: Floris Books.

-Laszlo, E. (1995). The interconnected universe: Conceptual foundations of transdisciplinary unified theory. London: World Scientific.

-Laszlo, E. (2004). Science and the Akashic field: An integral theory of everything. Rochester, VT: Inner Traditions.

-McTaggart, L. (2002). The field: The quest for the secret force of the universe. New York: Quill/HarperCollins. -2007.

-Ring, K & Cooper, S. Mindsight: Near-death and out-of-body experiences in the blind (II ed.) iUniverse Bloomington Indiana (First edition published 1999).

-Tarnas R. , Cosmos and Psyche: Intimations of a New World View, by Richard Tarnas, Penguin Group 2006.

-Wilber K. , The Spectrum of Consciousness, Quest Wheaton, 1977.

-Wilber K. , Up from Eden, Doubleday/Anchor, New York, 1981

-Wilber K. , A Social God, Mc Graw-Hill, New York, 1982

-Wilber K. , The Holographic Paradigm and other paradoxes, Shambhala, Boston, 1982.

-Wilber K. , Engler J. , Brown D. P. , , The Transformation of Consciousness, conventional and contemplative perspective on development (Shambhala Boston and London)1986 Shambhala Publications Inc.

-Wilber K. The Atman project: A transpersonal view of human development. Wheaton, Ill. : The Theosophical Publishing House 1980.

-Wilber K. , A Brief History of Everything, Shambhala Publications, 2000

-Wilber K. , Integral Psychology, Shambhala Publications, 2000

Primordial Psyche: A reliving of the Soul of Ancestors: a Jungian and Transpersonal Worldview.
by Diego Pignatelli

Primordial Psyche might be useful for any clinical research to the new approach to psychosis and the ancestral mind.Developing and expanding a Jungian perspective Diego Pignatelli brings new invaluable insights to psychotic phenomena and its ancestral prototype: the ancestral brain.

Through a Jungian framework, Pignatelli discusses borderline psychoses and schizophrenic phenomena which have their ancestral roots in a wide range of unconscious and numinous phenomena originating in the collective unconscious. He examines fascinating areas such as ethnology, shamanism, transpersonal psychology, anthropology, tantra,Hinduism,and primitive folk psychologies, Pignatelli sheds new light on the connection between the Reptilian Brain, spiritual and visionary experiences and Jungian psychology.

Primordial Psyche is a remarkable book, covering a range of spiritual phenomena from indigenous folk psychologies and pagan rituals to visionary revelations and magical thinking. It is rooted in Jungian thought but supplements it with a cogent analysis of disruptions in the modern psyche that are apparent in contemporary religious dogmas. Diego Pignatelli demonstrates the insights that have made him one of today's most original writers on the complexities of the human psyche.

-Stanley Krippner, Ph.D., Professor of Psychology, Saybrook University Co-author, *Extraordinary Dreams and How to Work with Them*

Diego Pignatelli sheds healing light upon the so-called disorders of the psyche that psychiatry tries to deal with, but only from within their medical model. Primordial Psyche gives us important spiritual perspectives on the full spectrum of human experiences that, let us hope, can be made of by clinicians everywhere to help more and more people reach their full potential, including our own.

Stuart Sovatsky, PhD , Author, *Words From the Soul*

"I find Diego Pignatelli's work a fine synthesis of transpersonal psychology, the mystical tradition, and analytic psychology. I am grateful that people like Pignatelli are doing the hard work of bringing these critical threads together in an analytic, synoptic perspective on modern personal and cultural life".

James Hollis Ph.D.,internationally renowned Jungian analyst and Author,Vice-President Emeritus of the Philemon Foundation, and director Jungian study program at Saybrook University,San Francisco CA.

INDEX

D

daimon 7
daimons vii, 46
damaru 36
de-Christianisation 5
defence mechanisms of projection
    and separation 65
demons 18, 34, 44, 67, 68
denial and identification in
    schizophrenic psychoses 65
devanagari 41, 44
Devil 18
Dhiti 42
differential diagnoses 51
Dionysian celebrations 18
Divine v, 20, 38, 45, 46
Divine Crazy 46
Divine Mad 45
Divine Madness v, 45
dragon slayer 4
dreamy odyssey 7
DSM-IV (APA, 2000) 45

E

emotional 6, 15, 51
endogenous psychoses 50
endogenous schizophrenic psychoses
    50
entheos (god within) viii, 10
epiphenomenon of matter 48
Eros 46
exorcisms vii, 66, 67
exorcisms and its bloody sacrifices
    66
experiential identification (mystic
    fusion, Grof, 1988, 2000) 51
experiential systematic studies (Grof
    & Grof 1989, 2010) 52
expulsion of Adam from Eden 5

F

fall of angels 5
Fracasso, Cheryl MS v, xi, xv, 77
Franz, Marie-Louise von 74, 86
Freud, Sigmund xiv, 19, 72, 79, 84

G

Ganges 41, 43
Genius 62
God xii, 10, 13, 14, 18, 40, 41, 46,
    55, 95, 100
Great Individual 4
Greyson, Bruce 27, 80, 91

H

hallucinatory 68
Hansen, G. 27, 92
Hercules 5
hero viii, xiii, xiv, xv, 2, 4, 5, 7, 11,
    12, 16, 17, 46, 62, 69
hero journey viii
hieros gamos 15
Hillman, James 92
Hindus 14, 29, 39, 40
holistic viii, xiii, 27, 50
Hollis, James 102
Holographic Mind v, 57
holographic model of the brain 49
holographic process 57
holography of the brain 57
Holotropic Breathwork 53, 82, 97
holotropic material 50
holotropic method 50
holotropic orientation 52
holotropic therapy xiii
homeostatic balance 14, 15
Hridaya (heart of Shiva) 43
human consciousness 53, 64
humanity vii, viii, ix, x, xiv, 2, 5, 6,
    7, 11, 12, 17, 18, 29, 30, 45, 46,

V

W

Y

Z